Lines of Destiny

RIDER

Lines of Destiny

How to read faces and hands – the Chinese way

Kwok Man Ho, Martin Palmer
and Joanne O'Brien

Rider & Company
London Melbourne Auckland Johannesburg

First published in 1986 by Rider & Company Ltd, an imprint of Century Hutchinson Limited, Brookmount House, 62–65 Chandos Place, Covent Garden, London WC2N 4NW

Century Hutchinson Publishing Group (Australia) Pty Ltd
16–22 Church Street, Hawthorn, Melbourne, Victoria 3122

Century Hutchinson Group (NZ) Ltd
32–34 View Road, PO Box 40–086, Glenfield, Auckland 10

Century Hutchinson Group (SA) Pty Ltd
PO Box 337, Bergvlei 2012, South Africa

Phototypeset in Linotron Plantin
by Input Typesetting Ltd, London

Printed in Great Britain by
Redwood Burn Limited, Trowbridge, Wiltshire and
bound by Pegasus Bookbinding, Melksham, Wiltshire

ISBN 0 7126 12645

Contents

1

The Beliefs of Physiognomy

To a well-appointed suite in one of the main streets of Hong Kong a group of Mainland Chinese farmers come; to a small back room in New York go successful Chinese diplomats and businessmen; to a renovated Victorian building in Manchester, now opened as offices, comes a mixture of Chinese teachers, social workers, businessmen and restaurant owners. The furnishings in the different rooms will be remarkably similar. The charts on the walls will show simple outline sketches of faces, profiles and hands. All these visitors, and the thousands like them from other walks of life, have come to have certain questions answered for the men they are visiting are traditional Chinese fortune-tellers who use physiognomy and palmistry as their means of divination. Wherever there are reasonable-sized Chinese communities, there will be the practitioner of the arts of physiognomy and palmistry. For many Chinese people, their lives are made comprehensible and given meaning by their men.

Yet to the casual onlooker what is this but an apparently small, insignificant survival of Chinese 'superstition'. And so it has been viewed by outsiders for years. But this is too hasty a conclusion. Chinese physiognomy is in fact a fascinating and highly practical example of some of the most deeply held and important Chinese religious and philosophical truths. It is a repository of fables, legends and stories. It is a glass which faithfully allows those outside to see directly into traditional Chinese ideas and family structures. It is also a collection of much common sense. We shall explore in a moment the religio-philosophical aspects which physiognomy (the term we shall use to encompass both physiognomy and palmistry) so sharply illustrates. Scattered through the book you will find various legends and fables – some of which even change their meaning from one telling to another! Likewise the careful reader will find the outlines of traditional Chinese life faithfully reflected. The paternalistic hierarchy of China is found in the fact that most predictions are given only for men. While we have included some western faces, this is an obvious break with tradition to which our physiognomist colleagues agreed in the interests of making the book appeal to a wider readership. The Chinese custom of one family taking over an extra or unwanted child from another family is also reflected in our text, as on p. 127. The values of long life, material wellbeing and a large, happy family are constantly shown in the predictions. Readers will be able to find many other examples. In terms of common sense, there are many comments, drawing upon an unbroken tradition of over 2000 years of studying the human form, which are simply true and useful observations – like the colour and shape of skin of those who are using drugs.

In compiling this book we have used the three most popular and commonly used books of the art. To return to our fortune-tellers in Hong Kong, New York and Manchester: before them would be a small and well-thumbed pile of books. In these piles, and most thumbed, would be three books which were written during the last thousand years. The oldest is the *Ma-i*, most important of the three. Next comes the *Pa P'u Tzu*, and finally the eighteenth-century book known as the *Golden Scissors*. Most of what is contained in our book has been taken direct from the collective wisdom of these three classics of physiognomy. However, just as the visitors to a fortune-teller would expect a particular person to give a particular reading, so we have done the same. Kwok Man Ho is a practising fortune-teller. Through his many years of study under Buddhist and Taoist monks steeped in these arts he has become well known. It is his readings of and commentary on the *Ma-i*, *Pa P'u Tzu* and *Golden Scissors* which run as a thread through this book.

But let us now turn to what this all means, to why so many Chinese take this all so seriously.

The first thing to stress is that Chinese physiognomy is not to be seen as a kind of game, a series of potentially meaningful or potentially meaningless statements arrived at for no apparent reason. It is in fact a highly complex system based upon fundamental beliefs in Chinese religion, philosophy and culture. It is also a powerful and at times illuminating way of looking at some of these beliefs and seeing their practical consequences in everyday life.

Physiognomy does not appear to have been an indigenous tradition with roots in the earliest history of China – the Shang and Hsai periods, *c.* 2000–1000 BCE. It appears first amongst the Chinese in the fifth or sixth century BCE as very much the property of magic men who do not appear to be related to any particular philosophical or religious system (see chapter 2). That they became involved and accepted over the next few hundred years means that something within physiognomy must have struck a chord with existing beliefs. Perhaps a key to this is to be found in the concept of ancestor worship. Ancestor worship is ironically both one of the most well known and the least understood aspects of Chinese religious belief. It underlies every system that has sought to develop religious ideas within China, be that Confucianism, where ancestor worship became very largely its *raison d'être*; Taoism, where the theme is underplayed, but nevertheless is a fundamental principle; or even the Catholic Church in China which split on the whole issue of ancestor rites and whether they were worship or merely reverence.

The aspect of ancestor worship that is of interest to us is its idea of fate and the shaping of the lives of descendants. Putting it very crudely, there are two ways of looking at physiognomy as a system for ascertaining the nature and future of a person. First, if you believe in fate, predestination or karma and its resulting cycle of birth, death and rebirth, then naturally, just as the reborn person's social status or position is a result of forces beyond the individual but which express themselves in that individual's life, so similarly physical appearance will also be determined by such factors. The second approach is to say that that which is within a person, his or her deepest thoughts, fears, hopes and aspirations, naturally express themselves outwardly. A modern example of this is psychosomatic illnesses. These two approaches are the subject matter of this chapter.

Ancestor worship is the earliest religious system that had a concept of fate (or even of predestination) with which physiognomy would have come in contact. Put very simply, if a person follows the correct path and lives as the respected ancestors would wish him to live, then blessings will come upon both him and his family and his endeavours. Thus one can talk of there being a predetermined *way* which it is *possible* to *follow*. If, however, the individual or indeed the entire clan chooses to part from the ways of the ancestors and not to follow the virtuous path, then calamity, distress and ultimately destruction are to be expected. This concept applied as much to the ordinary family as it did to the ruler, frequently known as the Son of Heaven. Ancestor worship contains notions of fate upon which physiognomy might have fastened in order to make itself intelligible as a system to the Chinese in the declining era of the Chu dynasty (*c*. 600–300 BCE). The fundamental idea is that, while much is predecreed or fixed by heaven, there is, nevertheless, room for personal action and the utilization of information in order to change the future. This is the core principle behind the idea of *ming* which is well expressed in the following quotation:

> Certain specific incidents were beyond human power to avoid once they had been decreed by Heaven and certain lasting aspects of the personal endowment from Heaven could not be altered . . . , but generally speaking there was no predetermined blueprint that prevented a man from following the dictates of his evaluating mind; nor did any antecedent plan prevent action in accordance with the moral sense from aiding the establishment of an ordered society. Confucius summed it up neatly in the *Analects* by saying, 'A man can enlarge his Way, there is no Way that can enlarge Man.'[1]

It is into this framework that the understanding and use of the *I Ching*[2] should be fitted. This book, traditionally ascribed to the period *c.* 1000 BCE and reputedly with commentaries by Confucius, is the oldest book of divination that the Chinese possess. Yet it is not a book which tells you inextricably and unalterably what your fate will be. Rather, it operates by looking at those things which are within your personality, those factors which are beyond your control and those aspects which, if you so desire, you may change by action. In certain instances it warns you what will happen if you do not act. In other instances it tells you what will happen if you do act. This is the important difference between the Chinese concept of *ming* and the Western concept of Fate with regard to this period of Chinese history. There is always the idea that personal action can prevent, forestall or exacerbate aspects which have been preordained or decreed by Heaven. In the Western tradition, once the idea of predestination was allowed, any change in fate through the exercise of free will was impossible; witness Greek tragedy or Scottish Calvinism.

The way in which this idea of Heaven's decree yet Man's responsibility works out in practice is seen very clearly in the *Shu Ching* (*The Book of Historical Documents*). In 'The Books of Shang', in the section dealing with the rule of King P'an Keng (reputedly ruled *c.* 1400 BCE; the text probably dates from *c.* 400 BCE), there is an interesting illustration. P'an Keng is addressing his people, having just built a new capital, an act designed to ward off certain bad fortune which was likely to befall them from Heaven. However, he also makes this charge to his people:

> Were I to err in my government, and remain long here, my high sovereign, the founder of our house, would send down great punishment for my crime, and say 'Why do you oppress my people?' If you, the myriads of the people, do not attend to the perpetuation of your lives,

> and cherish one mind with me, the one man, in my plans, my predecessors will send down on you great punishment for your crime, and say, 'Why do you not agree with our young grandson, but so go on to forfeit your virtue?' When they punish you from above, you will have no way of escape. Your ancestors and fathers urgently represent to my high sovereign, saying, 'Execute great punishments on our descendants.' So they intimate to my high sovereign that he should send down great calamities.[3]

Here we see both the activity of Heaven and of the ancestors, the activity of virtue and lack of virtue, and the possibility that through reform and repentance these disasters or decrees can be averted.

With the coming of Confucius (*c.* 500 BCE) little changed except that in his teachings he urged humanity to follow the Way of Heaven through reverence to ancestors, respect to superiors and filial piety as a means of living out that which is desired by Heaven and thus avoiding that which will be decreed as punishment by Heaven. However, these statements must be put into the context of our earlier description of *ming* and the way in which *ming* sees a shaping of individual destinies by Heaven as well as by individual participation. The idea that elements of one's destiny can be discerned in one's body or face has a root that is very clear in Confucianism. We can be what our ancestors desire us to be. Just as we are physically descended from our ancestors and bear certain physical traits that display this, so also can we display a moral and ethical inheritance. The major Confucian thinkers scorned such notions as fundamentally untraditional and unChinese, but because of these elements lying nascent within Chinese thought, physiognomy was able, despite opposition, to establish itself fairly successfully in a relatively short period of time.

From an early point onwards, however, this selfsame philosophy of both decree and free will was used explicitly to argue against the validity of physiognomy's assertions about destiny and the face. There is a famous story originally told against physiognomy. It is worth repeating here because it was turned round and used as evidence for physiognomy in later writings, most notably in the *Ma-i*. The second version in which the emphasis has been altered is on pp. 129–30.

There once was an old monk who was very learned in the ways of physiognomy, and he had a young servant by the name of Sung Chiao. One day the old monk looked closely at the face of Sung Chiao and saw that he had only a month to live. Being a compassionate man, he dismissed the boy and sent him home to his family, telling him to spend at least a month on holiday. As the boy journeyed, knowing nothing of his supposed fate, he saw a group of ants floating helplessly downstream on a piece of wood. Using bamboo poles and straw, he built a bridge to the piece of wood and helped the ants to crawl ashore, thinking nothing of it other than that it had been an act called forth from his kind nature. He continued on his way. When the month was over he returned to his master's house. His master was amazed to see him still alive and asked him what had happened to him in the last few weeks. The boy told the story of his going home and how he had saved the ants. Then it was that the old monk realized that nothing was irreversibly fixed by Heaven, and that acts of compassion and of goodness could change anyone's future.

This story, as it is told here, shows how individual action can change fate and therefore how limited is the possibility, as the original protagonists saw it, of physiognomy being able to give a true reading of the future.

What effect did the rise of philosophical Taoism, as exemplified particularly by the *Tao Te Ching*[4] and the *Chuang Tzu*,[5] have upon these concepts? The answer is remarkably little. Many of the core ideas which lie behind philosophical Taoism were shared by the general philosophy that also produced Confucianism. Taoism and Confucianism were as Martha and Mary, the active political social manifestation and the mystical hermitical aspect of that core philosophy. However, with the *Chuang Tzu* the first intimations of reincarnation which were and are so important to physiognomy begin to appear. The famous verse is found in chapter 6 of the *Chuang Tzu*, known as 'The Great Supreme'. The text goes as follows:

> To have attained to the human form is a source of joy. But, in the infinite evolution, there are myriads of others forms that are equally good. What an incomparable bliss it is to undergo these countless tranformations![6]

While this text is interesting, its influence and indeed the influence of much of philosophical Taoism in its pure form upon the general Chinese population and culture should not be overstressed, and should certainly be seen in conjunction with the influence of religious Taoism which arose from the second century CE onwards.

The development of Confucian thought fused with elements of philosophical Taoism produced its most strange and yet most logical philosophical disciple in the figure of Wang Ch'ung who was writing in the early first century CE and was heir to much of the scepticism of Hsun Tzu. His belief in a predetermined pattern was partly derived from the inevitability of the Way or Tao but also was a result of his interpreting what he saw as being part of the natural order which constrained and controlled all life. As a result, he believed that the individual had little if any control over the way in which superhuman forces shaped or determined his life. Like his forerunner Hsun Tzu, Wang Ch'ung devotes an entire chapter to physiognomy. Unlike Hsun Tzu, this chapter lauds physiognomy as being a logical scientific methodology for determining by physical characteristics inward constitution and thus also destiny. While this semi-scientific, semi-philosophical approach was not continued by even his own disciples, nevertheless it marks, as we shall see in chapter 2, a shift from a total opposition by major philosophers to physiognomy as something untraditional, to an acceptance of its role in Chinese society and thus an attempt to comprehend and explain its basis.

One of the main attacks that was and still is mounted on physiognomy is the argument that by convincing people that something is going to happen to them it does indeed happen, because those concerned both expect and then set about causing it to happen. To this end the following story, one of the most clear and detailed descriptions of physiognomy in Chinese writing, makes interesting reading. It is taken from *The Records of the Three Kingdoms*, the official Confucian account of the period from 220 to 265 CE. It is a biography of Chu Chien-p'ing:

Chu Chien-p'ing was a native of P'ei-Kuo. He was a skilful practitioner of the physiognomic arts among the common folk, and the effectiveness of his techniques had been proven many times. When the Grand Ancestor of our dynasty was Duke of Wei, he heard about Chien-p'ing and summoned him to court to be a court gentleman. [His son, the future] Emperor Wen was serving as commander in chief, and there were over thirty retainers in his presence. Emperor Wen asked Chien-p'ing how long he could hope to live and then had him go about the room and make a physiognomic analysis of all the guests present.

'General,' Chien-p'ing began, 'Your lifespan should be eighty years, but at forty you will have a small crisis. Please take care to protect yourself.' He told Hsia-hou Wei, 'You will become a provincial governor. At the age of forty-nine you will face a crisis, but if you manage to survive it, you will live to be seventy and rise to the post of ducal attendant.'

He then told Ying Ch'u, 'Sir, at age sixty-two you will become a high attendant official and will face a crisis. A year before that happens, you will see an apparition of a white dog, but it will be invisible to the people standing around you.' Finally, Chien-p'ing told Ts'ao Piao, 'Sir, you will be occupying a vassal state and, when you reach fifty-seven, will become entangled in a military action. You should take care to prevent it.'

Originally, Hsun Yu and Chung Yu, both of Ying-ch'uan, were the most intimate of friends. Hsun died first, when his son was still in infancy. His friend Chung was naturally called to be executor of the estate and wanted to take Hsun's concubine. He wrote the following to someone: 'Hsun Yu and I together once had Chu Chien-p'ing do a divination for us. He told me then, 'Although Hsun Yu is your junior, in fact it is fated that you will be left to manage his affairs.' When I heard that, I joked with him, saying, 'I will get his concubine A-ying, and that's all!' What does it mean that now he has indeed died, and what I said only as a joke has come to be realized? Today I want to marry A-ying; clearly it would be a good thing to do so. When I think back to the subtle vision of Chien-p'ing, I realize that even T'ang Chu and Hsu Fu could have added nothing to his prophecy.'

During the seventh year of the Huang-ch'u reign [226 CE], Emperor Wen turned forty years old, and he was plagued with a grave illness. He told his attendants of the right and left, 'The eighty years of which Chien-p'ing spoke must have been half in days and half in nights. I now face the point of crossing.' In a very short while, he died.

Hsia-hou Wei indeed became governor of Yen province. Early in the last month of the year, when he was forty-nine years old, he fell ill. Recalling Chien-p'ing's words, he reasoned that his lot was in fact to die at this time, so he began issuing his last testament and making preparations for the funeral so that everything would be in order when the time came. But two or three weeks later, his health turned about, and he recovered, almost to his former strength. On the afternoon of the last day of the month, he had his recording clerk pour some wine, and then he said, 'The ailment from which I have been suffering has gradually subsided. Tomorrow morning when the cock crows, I will reach age fifty and the danger period in Chien-p'ing's prophecy will have passed.' But after Wei bade his clerk good night and closed his eyes, the illness began to stir again. In the middle of the night he died.

At the age of sixty-one, Ying Ch'u became a palace attendant. When crossing through the inner palace he suddenly spied a white dog. He asked the people around him, but not a single other person could see it. As a result of seeing this apparition, he began giving parties and chasing about on pleasure trips away from the capital. He gave himself over to drinking, and, after another year had passed, at age sixty-two, he died.

Ts'ao Piao was enfeoffed as the king of Ch'u, but at age fifty-seven he conspired against the emperior with Wang Ling. When his plot was discovered, Ts'ao was ordered to commit suicide.

In explaining the fates of this entire group, Chien-p'ing never missed the mark. But I am not too clear on some of the details, so I have just recorded the rough outlines of several events. Only in the prophecies of the minister of works, Wang Ch'ang, the general of the northern expedition, Ch'eng Hsi, and the major general Wang Su, were there discrepancies. Su was sixty-two years old when he became critically ill. All his doctors felt that nothing could be done to save him, so his wife asked if he had any last words. Su said, 'Chien-p'ing predicted that I would pass seventy and that I would rise to occupy one of the three ducal posts. Now none of this has come to pass, but I for one will not have to worry about it.' Then he finally died.[7]

As can be seen, the writer, while acknowledging the prowess of Ch'u, nevertheless maintained the traditional Confucian historian's doubts about the validity of this kind of divination, and expresses his doubts in a most tactful way at the end of the section.

The Influence of Buddhism

As has been mentioned earlier, one of the most logical systems of thought that supports the viability of physiognomy is Buddhism with its teaching of rebirth. Many of those who now practise physiognomy professionally, that is to say Chinese physiognomists, are in fact lay Buddhists or Buddhist monks and nuns. For them physiognomy is a particularly powerful assertion of Chinese teachings about rebirth. The core teaching about rebirth and about karma – the effect which you build up through actions in one life and which carries forward into another – is nicely captured in a story told of Fa Hien, the great Buddhist monk who travelled to India to collect Buddhist sutras. On one occasion he was cutting rice with many of his fellow disciples when hungry thieves came and tried to force them to hand over their rice. The other monks fled, but Fa Hien stood up to the thieves and rebuked them roundly, saying, 'If you must have the grain, take what you please. But sirs, it was your former neglect of charity which brought you to your present state of destitution; and now, again, you wish to rob others. I am afraid that in the coming ages you will have still greater poverty and distress; – I am sorry for you beforehand.' And with those words he went away, and the thieves slunk off leaving the grain.[8]

What you do now will affect the birth you have later. What you did in previous lives has shaped what you are now. This is most harshly expressed in Chinese Buddhist belief and thus in physiognomy generally by the teaching that any physical handicap that you are born with now is an expression of wickedness in a former life – not bad enough to cause you to be reborn as a lower creature but certainly bad enough to cause you to be marked with a sign of your earlier actions. Given that one of the major ways in which your karma expresses itself is in the bodily manifestation that you will have in your next life, it is only natural that physiognomy should have developed as a system to explain how this operates. Of course, in the case of China it was the other way round, in that Buddhism arrived to find physiognomy already developed as a system with an implicit and at times an explicit philosophical basis. However, there can be little doubt that physiognomy also found in Buddhism a powerful logical and philosophical basis, and that it favoured this above all others as its system of thought. Thus it is that the story we told earlier about Sung Chiao and his act of mercy was able to be turned around in Buddhist thinking and made into a vehicle for physiognomy, as it is now used (see pp. 129–30). Buddhism teaches that while karma determines the form of life that you have now, and to a very great extent shapes the kind of life you have now, nevertheless acts of mercy and compassion can change that fortune. For this reason Ch'en T'uan, the great Sung philosopher and physiognomist, could argue that the future, while being shown in the face and body, bones and complexion, etc., can also be affected and changed by a person's heart. Through a good nature, bad karma can be transformed, but a good nature will always express itself physically in the demeanour of the face, the posture and shape of the body. Thus two apparently contradictory elements are held together in creative tension in physiognomical philosophy. Yes, you are what you are to a great extent because of what you have been. Yet you can use what you have to improve your karma and thus change to some extent your future, like Sung Chiao and P'eng Cho (see p. 47) who lived to a great age instead of dying as boys. Your previous actions and your present nature are both expressed physically. Your basic shape and mien are dictated by your karma. Yet a good heart can change that karma and will also manifest itself in your face, body and to a great extent in your hand.

The fusion of early non-Buddhist Chinese physiognomical thought – namely *ming* – and Buddhist concepts of karma and rebirth means that Chinese physiognomy, like Chinese divination using the *I Ching*, is not fatalistic in a Western way. It is so easy for people to use predestination as a means of avoiding personal or even corporate responsibility. The West in recent years has often displayed a disturbing use of non-Western fortune-telling techniques as a means of shunning responsibility by appeal to the inevitability of fate. This fatalism, which undoubtedly exists as a possibility in Chinese physiognomy and in other forms of Chinese divination, is not how Chinese physiognomists or diviners themselves interpret or use the system. This is an important point to bear in mind, for just as the *I Ching* does not tell you what inevitably will happen, so physiognomy does not tell you what inevitably will happen. Both systems indicate how, according to the way in which you are at the moment and have to some extent been created, you are likely to end up. However, by the exercise of free will, compassion, mercy, by invocation for the help of Boddhisattvas or by other acts of transcendental communication, that future can be changed. The important thing to bear in mind is that physiognomists do not see this as a failure of their system, rather as a justification of it. For all such changes will manifest themselves outwardly on the body often long before they are discerned in other ways.

In engaging in this sweep through early thought about physiognomy we have sought to show the core concepts that lie behind the idea that physiognomy can be a true science or art. Although there have been refinements and alterations to these basic ideas over the centuries, by the end of the T'ang dynasty, when Buddhism and Taoism had established to a large degree the mutual relationship which has persisted to this day, the main theoretical aspects or philosophical dimensions of Chinese physiognomy had been established. The unanimity between such major studies on physiognomy as the *Ma-i*, the *Golden Scissors* and the *T'ai-ch'ing Shen Chien* shows how little has really altered since the T'ang dynasty. The fact that to this day these books are the fundamental texts of practitioners of physiognomy shows the respect which they have been given, their relevance to modern divination, and the way in which they have satisfactorily answered the fundamental allegations levelled against physiognomy in religio-philosophical terms.

Physiognomy and Aspects of Traditional Chinese Belief

Having examined the more philosophical basis of Chinese physiognomy, we must now direct our attention to physiognomy's use of practical ideas found throughout Chinese religious practice. Of these, the three most important are the Five Elements; the Five Sacred Mountains; and the triad of Heaven, Man and Earth.

Without an understanding of these terms and of their centrality in Chinese belief, much which follows will be largely incomprehensible.

THE FIVE ELEMENTS

The Five Elements are, as their name suggests, the constituent elements of the world. In Chinese myths of the creation, the T'ai Chi or Ultimate divides into yin and yang, commonly expressed as light and dark, male and female, and so on. From these spring the Five Elements and the four seasons, and from these all that is is made. Therefore human beings, as much as any other physical manifestation of creation, bear within them the Five Elements. According to the Confucian or neo-Confucian philosopher Chu Hsi (*c.* 1180 CE), the Five Elements – metal (sometimes given as gold), earth, fire, water and wood – are not to be identified with the specific physical phenomena whose names they bear. Rather, the nature of each is regarded as being best defined by the element from which it takes its name. In classical Western thought there are four elements – water, air, fire and earth.

The Five Elements are reputed to be of great antiquity and are seen as having been given or revealed in the earliest time of Chinese history. They are found as a basic structure in all aspects of classic or ancient Chinese thought, and we can see them at work in physiognomy.

In order to comprehend their use and meaning in physiognomy, we must understand how they interrelate. This is best set forth in table form, thus:

Water	produces wood	but extinguishes fire
Fire	produces earth	but melts metal
Metal	likes water	but chops down wood
Earth	produces metal	but soaks up water
Wood	produces fire	but uses up earth

De Groot expresses this in traditional succinct fashion as follows:

> Wood produces fire, fire produces earth (i.e. ashes), earth produces metals, metals produce water and water produces wood (viz. vegetation) [and so on endlessly].
>
> Wood overpowers earth, earth conquers water, water vanquishes fire, fire conquers metal, and metal overpowers wood.[9]

The relationships set out above are considered as either positive or negative in physiognomy. Hence, a water-shaped person with a fire nature will have a predominently water-type personality as the fire element will be subservient to the dominant water nature.

THE FIVE SACRED MOUNTAINS

Among the earliest of Chinese beliefs is that of the Five August Rulers and their Sacred Mountains. These rulers and mountains express the cardinal points of the Chinese compass and the cardinal colours. The five cardinal points are south (which is placed at the top, unlike Western compasses), north, west, east and centre. These mountains, such as Mount T'ai in the south, have always been centres of pilgrimage and continue to be so to the present day. To the cardinal points the following mountains and rulers are ascribed:

Centre	Yellow Emperor (Huang-ti) at Sung Shan or Central Peak in Honan)
South	Red Emperor at Heng Shan or Southern Peak in Hunan
West	White Emperor at Hua Shan or Western Peak in Shensi
North	Black Emperor at Heng Shan (not the same as in 'South' – the characters are different but cannot be easily distinguished in sound) or Northern Peak in Chihli
East	Green Emperor at the most famous, T'ai Shan or Eastern Peak in Shantung

In traditional Chinese thought the known world was dominated by these five mountains – the highest points of the earth reaching to Heaven. It follows, therefore, that the plane of the face should be seen as dominated by the five mountains of the forehead, cheeks, nose and chin, the five most prominent features.

THE TRIAD OF HEAVEN, EARTH AND MAN

One of the most fundamental assumptions of Chinese religio-philosophical as well as mystico-magical thought is of the special and power-filled relationship between Heaven, Earth and Man. It is well captured in this phrase from the *Shu Ching*: 'Heaven and Earth are the father and mother of all creation; and of all things man is the most highly endowed spiritually.'[10] Likewise, in the equally ancient Classic, the *Li Chi (The Record of Rites)* is found the following: 'Of all creatures born of Heaven and nourished by Earth there is none greater than man.'[11]

The core belief lying behind the power of this triad of Heaven, Earth and Man is outlined in the first quotation above. It is the belief that Heaven and Earth are father and mother of all that exists, and that Man is the greatest fruit and fulfilment of that union. The dualistic struggle and harmony of yin and yang – female and male – finds concrete expression in Earth and Heaven, and Man is the key to the holding in creative tension of these cosmic forces. Thus in classic Chinese thought it is humanity which by its wrongdoings brings about both human and natural disasters, or by its virtuous actions sustains and furthers the creative fusion of yin and yang.

Within this overall scheme the Emperor as the supreme Man stood before Heaven and Earth as the symbol of all humanity. He it was who had to perform acts of repentance or contrition when the world of nature showed its displeasure at humanity's actions. This was traditionally done at the Temples of Heaven and Earth in the Imperial capital. For this reason the Emperor was known as the Son of Heaven. This scheme of things is captured in a section of *The Record of Rites* where Confucius is describing the nature of a truely wise ruler. 'The Son of Heaven forms a triad with Heaven and Earth. Thus in power of his goodness he is their correlate, and his benefits extend at once to all things. . . . When all things in the workings of Heaven and Earth that might be injurious are taken out of the way, we have the condition of righteousness.'[12]

The power of Heaven and Earth is attested to in many hundreds of popular quotations which are still in use today. More significantly, it is found in the most important festivals and events of the Chinese calendar, such as on New Year's Day when the Almanac, the *T'ung Shu*,[13] gives the instructions to worship Heaven, Earth and the ancestors. But it is also attested to by the use of Heaven, Earth and Man as the three most fundamental divisions in the physiognomy of the face. For just as in the popular saying 'Man is Heaven and Earth in miniature', so the face is the fate of the person in miniature. By studying the face it is believed that the fundamental forces in the universe can be seen as they accord to the particular destiny of the individual.

2
The History of Physiognomy

The history of Chinese palmistry and physiognomy is a fascinating one as, unlike most of the ancient arts of China, it cannot be traced back to the earliest – mythological – times. In the case of the *T'ung Shu* – the ancient Chinese Almanac – and its calendrical science, traditional medicine,[1] the *I Ching*'s hexagrams, geomancy, and so on, legend places their origins with the Three August Ones or the Five August Rulers – roughly *c.* 3000–2000 BCE. It is almost standard procedure that the origin of any distinctive Chinese art is ascribed to such mythological bringers of civilization as Fu-hsi, first of the Three August Ones, or Huang-ti, greatest of the Five August Rulers. That physiognomy does not claim such antecedents is an important clue to its history within China. Recent research on magical and divinational arts during the Han dynasty (207 BCE–220 CE) points to a growth of non-traditional arts stimulated by the advent of non-Chinese shamans and religious practitioners from other ethnic or cultural groups. For instance, De Woskin, talking of the diviners and magicians known collectively as *fang-shih*, says:

> During the early Han (221 BCE–9 CE), *fang-shih* were agents of a dramatic diffusion of non-traditional knowledge and interests into the highly centralized, literate, and essentially conservative court mainstream. . . . Unassimilated cultures from remote areas, notably Yen and Ch'i (Shantung), the I regions (Szechwan) and Ch'u (Yangtze river valley) were introduced and promoted, and practices associated with lower social strata (notably exorcistic and other mediumistic practices performed by priests among the populace) were elevated into court use.[2]

Here perhaps is the key to the origin of physiognomy within mainstream Chinese culture. It was certainly well enough established to rank as one of the skills of *fang-shih* and to attract crisp criticism from the philosopher Hsun Tzu in the third century BCE (as we saw in chapter 1). Yet the earliest figures cited by physiognomists in their histories are not to be found before the fifth century BCE. The lack of any link with the great mythological progenitors of Chinese culture, combined with the relatively late appearance of specific physiognomical practitioners, leads us to conclude that this art was introduced into mainstream Chinese culture between the sixth and third centuries BCE. This introduction came about as the result of non-Chinese religious figures and traditions coming into intimate contact with the various ruling houses of the Chinese home area through the expansion of different Chinese states into areas which had previously been largely unaffected by the Chinese. It is impossible to say with any certainty where such practices came from, but the most likely areas are either the extreme west, an area in contact with the Ch'in state, or in the southwest, which was in contact with or overrun by the mighty Ch'u state. The reason for excluding the north is that shamanism was the major expression of religion in this area, and there is no evidence of physiognomy being used by shamans. Beyond this it is impossible to go; the evidence is simply not there. Albeit, when physiognomy did enter, it appears to have done so with a particular flourish, in the company of other 'magical' arts and to the stern disapproval of the early Confucians.

The earliest figure cited by physiognomy books and tradition is the master known as the Devil Valley Master – Kuei Ku Tzu. He is reputed to have lived in the fifth to fourth centuries BCE and to have been the adviser to the two major statesmen, Su Ch'in and Chang I. Kuei Ku Tzu is referred to in this role by Ssu-ma Ch'ien in the *Shih Chi (Records of the Historian)*.[3] A book known as *Kuei Ku Tzu* still exists. It is a composite text, parts of which possibly date back to the fifth to fourth centuries BCE, and a strange mixture of magic, mysticism and philosophy. Kuei Ku Tzu's name is also linked with another book. This is the earliest book of fate divination extant and comes from the T'ang dynasty (618–906 CE). It is the *Li Hsu-chung Ming Shu* (*The Book of Fate of Li Hsu-chung*). In his preface Li Hsu-chung (*c.* 760–840) records that the core of his material was originally written down by Kuei Ku Tzu long, long ago.

So who or what was the Devil Valley Master? The title itself should give us some clues for it speaks of a powerful exorcist or practitioner of the occult arts. Yet he was also revered and noted as an adviser of statesmen. Perhaps this should not surprise us too much, for even during the Second World War Chinese statesmen and generals consulted such supernatural devices as the planchette – a two-handled stick which is 'controlled' by spirits and writes messages in a tray of sand. It would appear therefore that Kuei Ku Tzu fulfilled this double role of occultist and policy adviser. Although he may not have been the first to use physiognomy, his prowess in fate calculation and in statesmanship earned him a grudging respect from the Confucianist historians and statesmen such as Ssu-ma Ch'ien. In this way a model of considerable significance for the status of other practitioners of magic arts was established.

It is possible that opposition to physiognomy arose very early on in its first contact with Chinese culture. For instance, it is not inconceivable that the use of physiognomy by 'false' advisers lies behind the rebuke given by the Duke of Chou to the new Emperor. The text probably dates from the Han dynasty or even later but may contain original fragments. Talking of the practice of the 'founder of the Hsia dynasty' (1994–1523 BCE) of choosing men who he knew were 'thoroughly proved and trustworthy in the practice of the nine virtues' as administrators, the duke urges:

> With our heads to our hands and then to the ground, O Sovereign, we would say: Let such an one occupy one of your high offices. Let such an one be one of your pastors. Let such an one be one of your lawgivers. By such appointments you will discharge your royal duty. If you judge by the face only, and therefrom deem men well schooled in virtue and appoint them, then those three appointments will all be occupied by unrighteous people.[4]

Two of the earliest and best-documented accounts of physiognomists at work come from the era of the Warring States (480–221 BCE). The first of these physiognomists is Ku-pu Tze Ch'ing whose advice was sought by the King of Chin regarding his successor. To the amazement of all the other advisers, Ku-pu Tze Ch'ing, having examined the favourite candidate, rejected him, saying, 'His mother is but a vile slave-woman from Ti'. Instead he chose Chao Siang-tze who in fact succeeded to the throne and proved a powerful, assertive ruler.[5]

In the second early case Ssu-ma Ch'ien records in Ts'ai Tse's biography how he visited the physiognomist T'ang Chu. Ts'ai Tse asked for a prognostication. T'ang Chu, having given him a brief examination, then laughed and answered, 'Sir, you have a big nose, thick eyebrows, high shoulders, a domineering air, and weak knees. I have heard it said that superior men do not consult physiognomists – why don't you follow their example?' To this Ts'ai Tse answered, 'Wealth and honour I have, but I do not know how long I shall live. Please tell me what your art says.' T'ang Chu replied, 'Sir, you still have forty-three years to live.' Ts'ai Tse thanked him and left smiling. This took place in 306 BCE.[6]

While the above are fascinating glimpses – not least in the story of T'ang Chu – of how Chinese culture was still strongly resisting this new art, it is at the end of the period of the Warring States that we come to a fuller description. The most instructive account comes from an archenemy of physiognomy – the philosopher Hsun Tzu (*c.* 312–230 BCE). Hsun Tzu was disgusted at what he saw as a decline in religious behaviour and the foolish pursuit of superstition. In his book, known as *Hsun Tzu*, he devoted an entire chapter to attacking physiognomy (chapter 5). In so doing he has preserved for us, in negative terms, a picture of what third century BCE physiognomy taught. It is worth quoting portions of it for the details it gives:

> Formerly there were no physiognomists, and the word is not found in any books. Ku-pu Tze Ch'ing . . . and T'ang-Chu . . . began to examine the appearance, the stature and the complexion of persons, in order to deduce therefrom their good or evil destiny, and whether they would live a long or short life. Ignorant folks believed such nonsense, but in ancient times the practice was quite unknown, and books make no mention of it. It would be much better to speak of the heart rather than examine the countenance, better still to discourse on men's intentions rather than on the heart, for the heart is better than the countenance, and a man's intention better than the heart itself. If the intention is upright, the heart is likewise good.
>
> Even if a man's appearance be against him, but the intention of his heart is good, he is a superior man. On the contrary, given a man enjoying all exterior advantages, if his intentions are perverse, he is a worthless individual. There is nothing more desirable than to be a superior man, and nothing more despicable than to be a worthless person!
>
> Therefore, a man's exterior, be he of high or low stature, gaunt or stout, gifted with fine features or ugly as a toad, exerts utterly no influence upon his good or evil fortune. The Ancients never noticed such twaddle, and writers did not even mention it in their books.
>
> Chow, Chou-Kung . . . was of low stature. The head of Confucius, K'ung-tze, . . . was much depressed; Duke Chou, Chou-kung, . . . was stiff and stood bolt upright like a piece of decayed wood; Kao-yao, . . . High Minister to Yao . . . and Shun, . . . had features like a parched melon; Hung-yao, . . . disciple of Kiang Tzu-ya . . . and minister to Wu-wang . . . (1115–1078 BCE), was so beardy that his features were almost concealed; Fuhyueh, . . . whom Wu-ting-wang, . . . one of the emperors of the Yin . . . dynasty, chose as minister (1324–1265 BCE),

resembled a fish standing up; I–yin, . . . High Minister to the emperor Ch'eng-t'ang, . . . who subdued the tyrant Kieh, . . . XVIIth and last ruler of the Hsia . . . dynasty, was beardless and destitute of eyebrows.

The emperors Kieh . . . and Chow . . . were well built and of commanding stature; they were, notwithstanding, but tyrants. Endowed with Herculean strength, they had enemies on all sides, and ruined themselves as well as the empire. They were monsters of cruelty, and their names have been handed down to posterity as symbolical of all tyranny. It is not, therefore, the countenance which injures a man, but the lack of prudence and intelligence which causes his misfortune. Who among the crafty and cunning folks of our large cities has not pleasing and well-set features?

Ask physiognomists which is preferable, a pleasing countenance or upright intentions, for it is not the features that injure a man, but his lack of prudence and intelligence.[7]

It is interesting to note how Hsun Tzu's first attack on the whole art is based upon its lack of Chinese ancestry – its newness within Chinese culture and language. We have discussed the concepts and beliefs behind physiognomy and its detractors in chapter 1.

By the time the Han dynasty was established (207 BCE) physiognomy was settling down into the mainstream of Chinese life. Books such as the *I Wen Chih* were now devoted to physiognomy. But perhaps the most significant move was the acceptance of physiognomy on a religio-philosophical basis, as exemplified by the Taost-influenced Confucian philosopher Wang Ch'ung, probably the single most important Chinese philosopher in the momentous first millenium CE. We have discussed his views in chapter 1, but suffice it to say that, for entirely 'logical' reasons, Wang Ch'ung came out in favour of physiognomy as a science in his book *Lun Heng* (*Discourses Weighed*), *c*. 80 CE. With this blessing and the general growth of interest in magic as evidenced by the spread of popular religious Taoism in the late Han period, physiognomy was part of the fabric of Chinese life. It occurs quite naturally in the epic story of the disturbed Three Kingdoms period, both in the official histories as well as in popular accounts. Hence the tale – a favourite topic of temple paintings and celebrated in story and song to this day – of Liu Pei and Chu-ko Liang. Liu Pei was one of the chief agents of the demise of the Han dynasty, seizing power in Szechwan. He is best remembered as one of the three heroes of the immensely popular *Story of the Three Kingdoms*[8] where he appears alongside Kuan Yu, later deified as Kuan Ti, the God of War.

The story goes that once Liu Pei had taken control of his part of China he asked the famous divinator Chu-Ko Liang to become his adviser. Liang refused three times but eventually entered his service. He then predicted correctly, by reading Liu Pei's palm, the division of China into the three kingdoms.

The next major influence on physiognomy and palmistry is undoubtedly the introduction of Buddhism during the first five centuries CE. Buddhism began to penetrate China during the Han dynasty – legend places it *c.* 64 CE. Certainly by the third and fourth centuries CE Buddhism was a major phenomenon within Chinese religious, political and philosophical thought. Most of the major books or sutras of Mahayana Buddhism had been translated, and pilgrims such as Fa-hien were making their way from China to India in search of further Buddhist knowledge. The impact of Buddhism on palmistry and physiognomy was not that of radical transformation but, rather, lay in the provision of a more detailed and consistently worked-out philosophy. Palmistry and physiognomy were, of course, known within the Indian homeland of Buddhism and it is possible that certain techniques may have come across the mountains with Buddhism. However, judging from biographies of some of the physiognomists during the Han period, Chinese physiognomy seems to have needed little from Indian physiognomy and palmistry other than a deeper and more explicitly religious purpose behind its practice. This was to be found in the detailed understanding of reincarnation. At times Buddhist scholars have been not a little uneasy about the simplistic connection between Buddhism and various forms of divination which was often made by wandering monks who were not under the authority of any particular abbot. However, it can be seen from the following story that this relationship nevertheless reflected a reality both in the popular mind and in the way in which Buddhism became acceptable in China. The tale is told of a famous Buddhist monk of the fourth to fifth centuries called K'ang Seng-yuan who probably came from central Asia. He became so proficient in Chinese that he was often teased by his Chinese friends about the fact that he did not look Chinese. He is supposed to have responded to a particular comment about his deep-set eyes and high nose by saying, 'The nose comprises the mountain of the face, while the eyes are its springs. If a mountain is not high, it will not be famous. If a spring is not deep, its waters will not be clear.' Besides being considered a classic example of wit, K'ang Seng-yuan points out that regardless of race all that matters is whether the face gives a good physiognomical reading.

The ideas associated with physiognomy and rebirth which were implicit in the philosophy and writings of Wang Ch'ung, and which were then amplified by the rise of Buddhism, came under Taoist critique towards the end of the T'ang dynasty. Taoism found itself threatened by the rise of Buddhism and sought in particular to attack those aspects of Buddhist thought which it deemed to be unChinese. Amongst these was the idea of rebirth and in particular the assumption that what you are now is the direct result of what you had were previously. A Buddhist physiognomical response to this arose at the end of the T'ang and early Sung dynasties and is perhaps best exemplified by the famous and almost legendary figure of Ch'en T'uan, also known as He'yi. He is held up by present-day physiognomists, both Taoist and Buddhist, as one of the greatest physiognomists ever. Legend asserts that he studied under Old Master Ma-i – the reputed author of the *Ma-i*, one of the most influential and currently important books on physiognomy. The story goes that Ch'en T'uan went to study under Ma-i after Ch'en had rejected the life of the Court despite the pleas of the then Emperor, Tai Tsung. Ch'en sat at the feet of Ma-i in a small stone hut high in Hua Shan, one of the Five Sacred Mountains (see p. 19). The core of the teaching that Ma-i gave to Ch'en was: physiognomy is not fixed by Heaven but you can know what a person will be. A person who is rich or noble, rich or gentle, who has long life or war, who is fortunate or kind or angry, all this appears on their surface. Also you can know this through their bones and complexion, voice and so on. Study this and you will know true physiognomy. But know most of all that a person's face is not fixed by the Gods and that the future depends on a person's heart. We have explored this idea in chapter 1.

From the Tang dynasty onwards numerous books were written regarding physiognomy. Of these, three are still of major significance in contemporary physiognomy. The first is the *Ma-i*, which is tentatively dated at the beginning of the Sung dynasty (*c*. 1000 CE). The second is the *Pa P'u Tzu*. Pa P'u Tzu was reputedly a wise man who lived during the Ming dynasty (*c*. 1400 CE) and wrote this book which contains the most detailed explanations of physiognomy. The third most significant book is the *Golden Scissors*, which dates from the early Ch'ing dynasty (*c*. 1700 CE). *Golden Scissors* contains much of the reputed history of physiognomy, along with the more recent, probably Ch'ing dynasty, introduction which first appeared in the *Ma-i*. There is little disagreement between the three books; rather, it is the detailed nature of their explanations which makes them of interest. The famous

French sinologist, Henri Doré, records in his notes on physiognomy that he drew most of his information from the *Ma-i* which he received as a gift from a practising physiognomist.[9] Indeed, it has been the practice generally that those interested in physiognomy are first given the *Ma-i* because it is seen as being historically the earliest of the three.

There is little else of historical significance regarding physiognomy in the period from the *Ma-i* (*c.* 1000 CE) to the present day. It is perhaps worthwhile glancing briefly at the impact of physiognomy as a system, particularly at times when traditional Chinese values were under major assault. For instance, during the nineteenth century, particularly the era of the T'ai-ping Rebellion, when values were under pressure from Western missionaries, traders and officials, as well as from rebels within China itself, many used physiognomy as the first means of judging a person's value. For example, Tseng Kuo-fan, who was responsible for the major resistance to the T'ai-ping Rebellion, often employed physiognomists and the ideas of physiognomy as a way of judging the likely behaviour of his officers. Indeed, at the end of the nineteenth century and in the early twentieth century his actions and his success were often attributed to his wisdom in physiognomy. A similar practice was observed in the Kuomintang period during the Japanese invasion of China (1931–45). According to C. K. Yang,

> In the momentous change of political fortunes, the old officials felt an even greater need for such supernatural guidance [such as physiognomy and palmistry] and consolation. Thus contemporary Confucian scholars believe in fate not only as a strengthening agent of the moral cause but also as a supernatural notion of pre-determinism in the course of human events.[10]

Since the coming to power of the Communists in China in 1949 traditional religious practices such as physiognomy have been under severe censorship. There can be no question that many of the abuses of physiognomy which attracted the condemnation of reformers of all kinds are exactly the kind of abuses which serious practioners of physiognomy would also wish to see eradicated – the deliberate attempts to fool people and misrepresent physiognomy amongst the illiterate masses. Furthermore, as we have seen, a critical tradition has been present within Chinese philosophical and religious life since at least 300 BCE, as exemplified in the figure of Hsun Tzu. Nor has that criticism remained silent during the long period when physiognomy was an accepted aspect of traditional Chinese life. Reformers have always pointed to it along with other forms of popular religious belief as being a block to a true understanding of life, whether that true understanding be Confucian, Moslem, Christian or Marxist.

However, it would be very foolish to conclude that physiognomy in China is now extinct or that interest in it has died. Indications are that, since the opening up of China and the greater ease with which information is now available, these practices have never died. For instance, an article in *New China News Agency* of 28 December 1982 refers to:

> so-called feudal superstitious activities primarily . . . unscientific, absurd activities, such as begging for the advent of Gods or immortals, practising planchette writing or divination, expelling ghosts in order to cure sickness, praying for rain and for an end to natural disasters, practising physiognomy and other fortune-telling tricks and practising geomancy.[11]

It is not clear whether major texts such as the *Ma-i* or *Golden Scissors* are still being published by Buddhist temple presses and other such groups. Although major Taoist and Buddhist works, that is to say the great scriptures, are officially published, it seems highly unlikely that any official approval has or will be given for such 'superstitious' books. However, rumours reaching observers in the West and current amongst Chinese practioners of physiognomy seem to indicate that the publication of such books has continued without serious interruption, albeit in an underground manner.

Given the eternal human fascination not only with one's own face and body but also with the future and with the past, physiognomy is unlikely to die out. Perhaps the greatest risk is that, in a situation where honest discussion and exchange of ideas between those who oppose it and those who support it cannot take place, much of the intellectual, philosophical and religious teaching that lies behind these practices will be lost or abused. It will then become but a hollow shell, an art without form, a philosophy without a meaning. For it must never be imagined that physiognomy in its major expression in China has ever been anything less than the logical working out of certain beliefs and understandings about the transcendent and the human; about the divine and the terrestrial; about birth, death and what life holds after death.

3
The Five Elements and the Five Long or the Five Short

The Five Elements

In Chinese physiognomy there is a tradition of categorizing people according to the Five Elements. Everyone will match up with at least one of these categories. Most people are a combination of two or more elements; rarely do we find someone consisting of a pure element.

Even if we know someone's elemental combination we can only make a superficial judgement about his or her character and fortune, since we have to take into account evidence from the rest of the body. Thus, although it is possible to say a water-shaped person is intelligent, this would have to be double-checked by examining the head line on the palm of the hand (Figure 1). If the head line is deep and of average length, then we judge that this person is intelligent, but this is not the case for someone whose line is weak, broken, short or too long. The reading of the head line can apply to all the Five Elements.

Someone whose head line slopes downwards (Figure 1 – a) only enjoys friendship, art and writing. A head line which is straight indicates a concern with money and an eagerness to gain material rewards (Figure 1 – b). If your head line rises towards the little finger you are not only avaricious but also ruthless in how you acquire money (Figure 1 – c).

Someone with a line sloping down will find a career in the arts or in academia, as an author for example, or a singer, an actor or a lecturer. A head line that is straight or rising signifies a career in

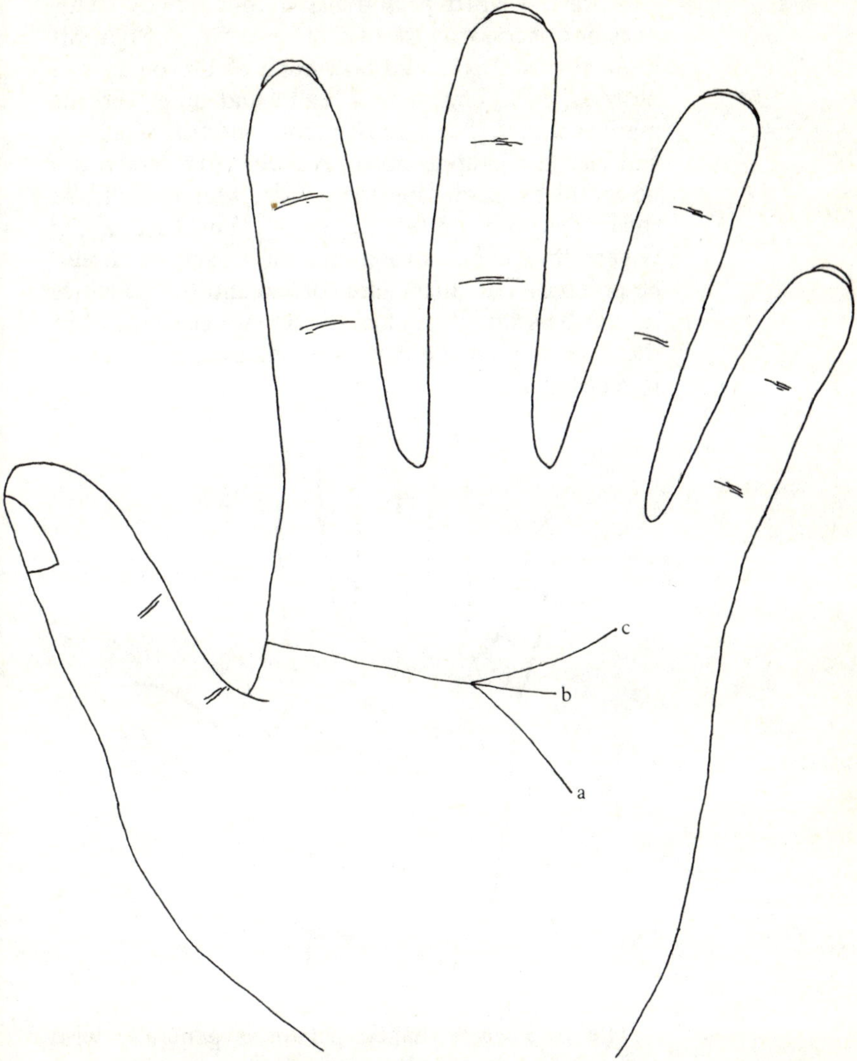

Figure 1

commerce; such a person's main concern will be the size of his salary. The most suitable career for those with the latter types of line is a disciplined one such as the armed forces, the police or politics.

WATER SHAPE

The water-shaped person has a round body. This does not necessarily mean that he is fat, but that his limbs are well rounded and none of the bones can be seen. His demeanour is calm and quiet and his manner direct. The skin is smooth and full of colour, and has an oily appearance. A true water person can be found by examining the hands, which should be thick, soft and tender (Figure 2). The base of the fingers should feel strong and the fingertips should be pointed. The fingers are conical and the knuckles cannot be seen. If the hand is not water-shaped but the face is, then the person is not considered to be water-shaped.

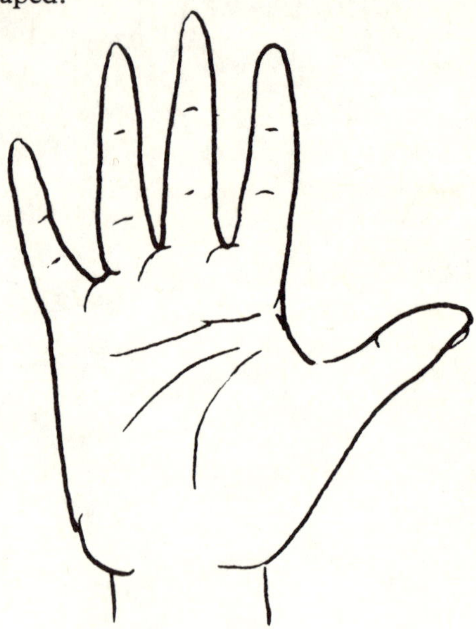

Figure 2

The true water-shaped person is generally wise and will become wealthy since he has an intelligent nature. According to the Chinese: 'If one is like water, one likes to study.' The true water-shaped person has a good head line; only by checking the shape of the hand and making sure that the head line slopes downwards can we determine if someone is a true water-shaped person (Figure 1 – a).

Such a person is difficult to find as usually other

elements which bestow good or bad qualities are mixed in his nature. Some elements complement each other perfectly while others clash; this will be reflected in the character and build.

Water Shape with Gold

The water shape favours a person who has some gold in his nature. This can be seen in the white colour of the skin and the square shape of the body. The combination of water and gold signifies good luck. A Chinese poem says, 'Water was born from gold, he will be famous and wealthy, to know is to be round, to be active is to be square.' Someone with a round body and a square face can look forward to good fortune. However, sometimes the gold nature is too heavy for the water shape; for example, someone with a round body, white skin, square face and sharp, high voice will be neither famous nor wealthy. He is likely to have few children or none at all. This is because too much gold produces muddy water. The correct balance for the water shape with a gold nature can be seen in someone with patches of white on a darker skin. Such a person sits calmly, acts slowly and methodically and has what is known as a square nature. If there is too much gold, then the skin is powder white, the muscles are thin, the bones can be seen and the veins stand out.

Water Shape with Earth

A water-shaped person with an earth nature will suffer from weak health and bad luck throughout his life. The Chinese have a saying: 'The water-shaped person with a heavy nature will be homeless and poor.' This combination can be seen in someone with a dry, yellow complexion, a strong build and heavy bones. However, a complexion with only slight tinges of yellow and a glossy, shining skin signifies no such difficulties in life.

Water Shape with Fire or Wood

A fire nature (red skin colour) or a wood nature (green skin colour) combines fairly well with a water shape. Such a person has no need to worry.

FIRE SHAPE

The fire-shaped person has a long head, wide chin and a domed forehead. The face is red and shiny, the hair or beard slightly brown, the ears pointed and the eyebrows rise upwards. The voice tends to be dry and rough, and the sinews and bones on the face and hands can be easily distinguished. The hands themselves are sharp and strong and the knuckles are bony (Figure 3). An ancient physiognomy book known as the *Fung Kam* says, 'To know the fire-shaped, look at the upper sharp and lower wide.'[1]

The nature of fire is politeness, therefore the fire-shaped person is well mannered but has a hot

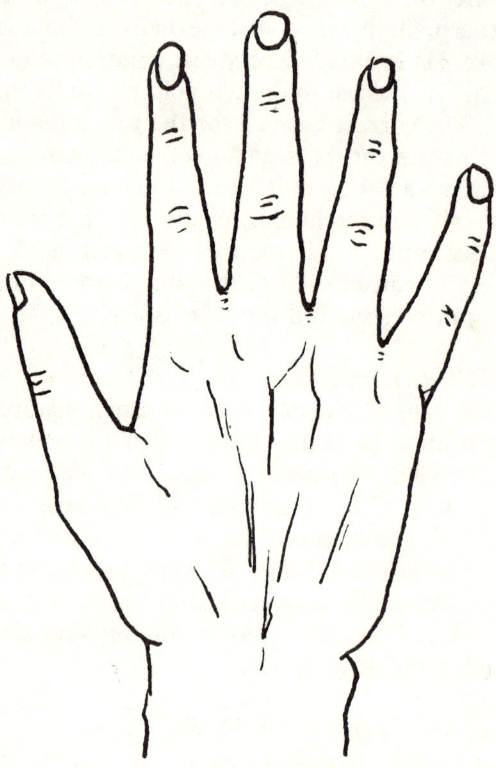

Figure 3

temper. He is suited to disciplined work such as the armed services and is likely to be successful before middle age, but can lose a position of power very quickly. Since fire flares up easily but eventually dies, so the fortunes of the fire-shaped person will fluctuate throughout his life. It is therefore best if the fire-shaped person has a wood nature, since wood fuels the fire and keeps the flames bright.

Fire Shape with Wood
Someone with this combination will have a clear voice, a thin straight body and bones which can be seen clearly. Success and fame are likely to arrive around thirty years of age, and will continue because of this mixed nature.

Fire Shape with Water
This is a bad combination since water easily extinguishes the fire, thus the two elements will never work harmoniously. The fire-shaped person with a water nature has a round build and a dark-coloured skin. The bones and the sinews cannot be seen. His relationship with his partner and children is troubled, and he will always have difficulty saving money.

Fire Shape with Earth
This combination can be seen in the yellow colouring of the skin and in the strong build, particularly in the shoulders and the back. The Chinese say that fire produces earth, so an earth nature has less strength and energy than a pure fire nature; however, this is not considered an unlucky combination. The good qualities of the true fire-shaped person will be present but not in such great quantities.

Fire Shape with Gold
It is very unusual to find this combination since it is very difficult to spot the white skin colouring and square shape of the gold nature against the dominant force of the fire element. You are more likely to find a gold-shaped person with a fire nature.

WOOD SHAPE

A wood-shape person is thin, tall and straight, with strong, hard joints and sinews. The hair and eyebrows are thick and the eyes are long and clear. The skin tends to have a green tinge. The waist is slim and hands are flat and long. The fingers are slim and the skin over the joints has a knotted appearance (Figure 4). When you examine the fingers you can see many small vertical lines. The true wood-shaped person has a kind nature and can expect a long life. Wealth will not arrive until late in life.

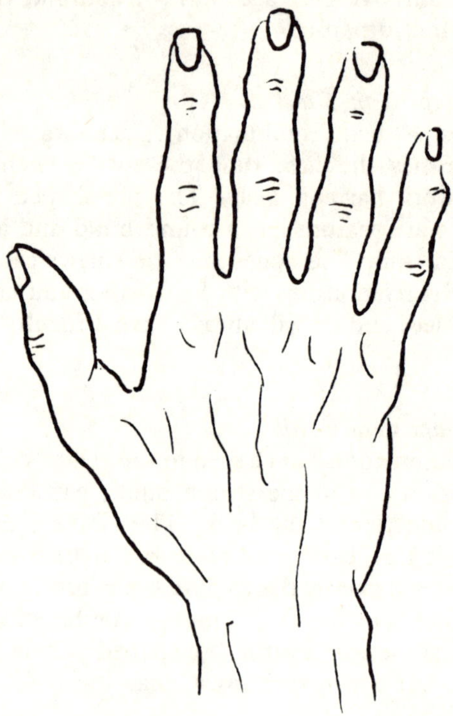

Figure 4

Wood Shape with Gold

The skin has a gold colour and the build is square. Ancient fortune-tellers say that people with too strong a gold nature will have difficulties in life;

although they work hard, they will earn little and are unlucky with money. This bad fortune will rub off onto their family and eventually lead to unhappiness in the home. It may even result in divorce or cause the children to argue with their parents and leave home. If a person has only a little gold in his nature he will be able to mould this to his wood shape and benefit from this mixture (as gold can be fashioned). Such a person is likely to be famous and rich.

Wood Shape with Water

This is the luckiest combination since water produces wood appearance. The ancient fortune-tellers said that wood and water stay together and will always be rich and noble. The wood-shaped person with a water nature is creative and likely to be talented in writing or in art. As long as the water element is not too strong many opportunities will come his way. Too much water means the wood will float and thus lose its value. The wood-shaped person with too much water will become fat and his skin will darken; as a result he will not enjoy the benefits that derive from a good balance of wood and water.

Wood Shape with Fire

The wood-shaped person with a slight fire nature will have good luck. Such a combination is easy to recognize since the face is red and the skin greasy or moist. The amount of fire does not matter since the growing pattern of fire is almost the same as that of wood.

Wood Shape with Earth

This combination is usually recognized by the mixture of green and yellow tinges in the skin colouring and the raised veins on the hand. These veins will not be as obvious as those of a wood-shaped person. This person will have quite a strong build, but the earth reduces the power of the wood. He will not be noted for his kindness, nor will he live as long as the true wood-shaped person.

GOLD SHAPE

The characteristics are a square shape and a white skin. The body is strong boned and the muscles hard and well formed. Weak bones and fatty muscles indicate an apathetic nature. If, after close examination of the face, the features are found not to be well balanced, then the person concerned does not have a true gold nature. The hand of the gold-shaped person ought to be square, the fingers strong and skin elastic (Figure 5). By nature he will be strong-minded, patient and sensible, and will stick to any decisions which he makes. He will tend to worry about work, and spend time on his business rather than becoming involved with hobbies. Such people concentrate on what is happening at a particular moment and do not while away their time on daydreaming.

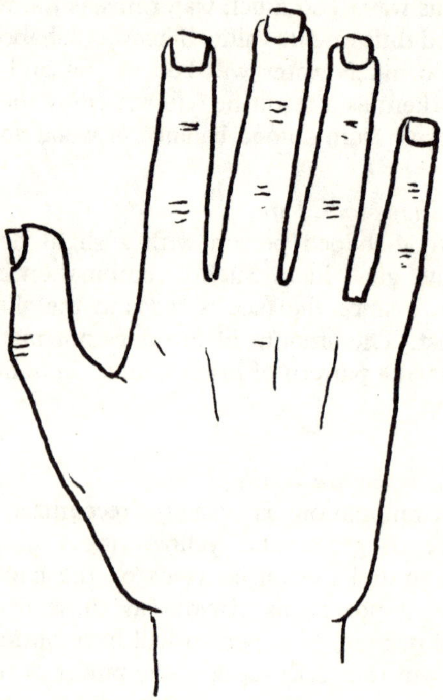

Figure 5

The sign of gold is reliability; those who have a gold shape will never forget a favour and can be trusted to keep a promise. During working hours they will work hard and abide by any rules. They will not tolerate mistakes, reporting any to their superiors. For this reason they are well liked by those above them. Away from work the gold-shaped person takes on a completely different character, becoming friendly and relaxed. Although straightforward in all his dealings, he will have difficulty making close friends since he is too honest. He does not like to mix with those of lower status and tends to be disliked by workmates who frequently complain about him. He is suited to a job in the law or in the armed forces since this gives him a disciplined, orderly life.

Gold Shape with Fire

Fire has the power to destroy gold; similarly a fire nature can destroy the gold-shaped person. This combination can be seen in prominent facial features and protruding bones. The skin has a red colour. Such a person will suffer misfortunes and will be involved in an accident or disaster one day. If the face is white with only slight traces of red, it means that this person has a light fire nature and is able to mould events to his benefit, just as a moderate fire can shape gold but not destroy it. The gold-shaped person with a light fire nature will not be fortunate in youth, but luck and wealth will come his way in middle age.

Gold Shape with Earth

This is a lucky mixture since it is earth which produces gold. The ancient fortune-tellers said that gold with thin earth enables the body to cope with jewels and fortune. Such a person is likely to have fruitful results from his work and will be successful in trading or planning. When the gold shape combines with earth the body is well built, the muscles are hard and the skin has a yellow colouring. However, too much earth in the nature is unlucky since earth can prevent gold from being found.

Gold Shape with Water
Whilst it is impossible to recognize this particular combination since the two elements are so completely different, it is nevertheless possible to have a water-shaped person with a gold nature.

Gold Shape with Wood
Since the wood shape is thin and the gold shape is large, it is difficult to recognize this mixture. The one feature where it is expressed is in the hands. The knuckles, sinews and veins can be clearly seen and they signify someone who may work hard but has difficulty attaining a high position in his job. As a result he will never be wealthy.

EARTH SHAPE

The features of the earth-shaped person are large and thickset. He has a big nose, wide mouth, thick lips, round chin, hard muscles and strong bones. The hands are thick, rounded, strong and muscular (Figure 6). The skin colour is golden-yellow and the voice is strong and loud. If the skin is pale grey and the muscles or the voice weak, this is not a true earth shape even though the other features are present. The life of such people will be difficult and they will never attain fame or fortune. They are honest, will earn little and try not to overspend. They are modest, loyal, trusting and hard-working even in the most difficult jobs. They are full of energy but tend to be adamant and speak their own mind. The sign of the earth nature is truth, and such people can be relied upon to keep a promise. They are skilful in their actions and adept at planning. It is difficult to uncover their thoughts. The true earth-shaped person is reliable and honest. He will be rich and live a long life.

Earth Shape with Wood
This is a bad combination since earth and wood jar against each other. Although the body is not thin, the veins can be seen clearly and the skin has a green

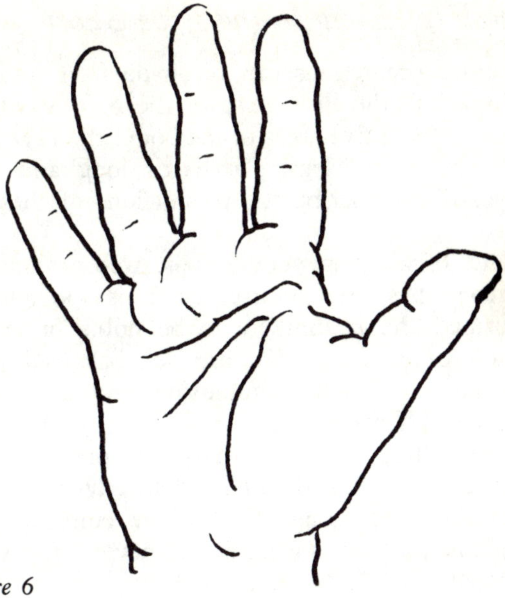

Figure 6

tinge. The earth-shaped person with a wood nature will be unsuccessful in his actions and poor throughout his life.

Earth Shape with Fire

This is a lucky mixture since fire warms the earth and helps it to maintain life. Such a person will have a red colour underneath a yellow skin, and will be fortunate and rich.

Earth Shape with Water

This mixture is rare but can be recognized by dark skin colouring combined with a traditional earth shape. People with this combination will have difficulties both with their career and in family relationships.

Earth Shape with Gold

This person is quite well built but not fat and has white to yellow skin colouring. Since earth has the capacity to produce gold, this is a lucky combination which signifies wealth and success.

The Five Long or the Five Short

Accurate predictions can be made from what the Chinese call the Five Long or the Five Short. The 'five' refers to five areas of the body: the head, face, body, hands and legs. The terms 'long' and 'short' are used to describe the proportions of these five areas.

The Five Long should look well balanced; if someone has one feature which is too short or deformed, he is unlikely to be noble or rich. A person whose Five Long are well balanced should also have a bright complexion and a vivacious character. If his complexion is dull and sleepy and his body limp, with the veins standing out on the surface of the skin, then he is not deriving any good from the Five Long. He will be employed in a mundane job and as a result will never know wealth or be successful.

Some variation in the proportions of the limbs is acceptable. For example, someone whose hands and arms are proportionately longer than his legs still has a chance to be rich, but if a person's arms and hands are obviously much shorter than his legs he is thought to have a very unlucky physiognomy. The ancient fortune-tellers predicted that a person with the latter proportions would sell everything he owns, lead an idle life and be disregarded by others. Those whose hands and arms appear long in proportion to their legs should never encounter insurmountable problems so long as they put effort into their work.

Someone with well-proportioned Five Short will also have a vivacious character and smooth muscles and bones. The *yin t'ang* (the area between the eyebrows; see pp. 98–106) should have a bright cast as though a light is shining from it. The Five Mountains of the face (see p. 122) should be in proportion to one another. Even if you have one feature which is larger than the others or slightly crooked, but which still fits in well with the shape of your face and is thought by others to be an attractive feature, your Five Mountains will be considered in proportion.

If the bone and muscles of your body are uneven or too pronounced and the Five Mountains are dented, scarred, hollow or crooked, then you will have great difficulty finding good opportunities. By nature such people have a dejected look and are slow to respond. The ideal Five Short person should have a small build with delicate bones. The *yin t'ang* should be flat or slightly rounded and the Five Mountains in proportion. The ancient fortune-tellers claimed that the eyebrows should be rounded, the eyes large, the forehead very full like a bear, the body long and the legs short. The aura emitted by the Five Short is that of an important leader.

In order to give a precise forecast, an examination of the Five Short should be complemented by a study of the face and the complexion. Just as unsightly foliage can detract from the beauty of a flower, so can bad features adversely affect the fortunes of a person with well-proportioned Five Short.

The Five Long usually accompany wood- or fire-shaped people; the Five Short are usually found in gold, water or earth shapes. If you make a reading of your body and face but are unsure how well balanced your features appear, then examine your eyes. Clear, bright eyes signify an alert, proud person who, even though poor, will not take charity or rely on others. (For how to make an informed examination of the face, see chapters 4–9.)

4
The Five Features: The Eyebrows

The five features are made up of the eyebrows, eyes, nose, mouth and ears. If any feature is not in harmony with the others – for example, a cut or damaged lip or one eye larger than the other – the balance of the five features is destroyed. Conversely, if four of the features are discordant but the fifth has a perfect shape and colour, then this will enhance your luck. The Chinese liken this combination to a drop of clean water which makes dirty water less murky.

Once again, the face cannot be examined in isolation from other parts of the body. All areas have to be inspected, good and bad aspects have to be evaluated; only then can an accurate prediction be made.

The Eyebrows

The Chinese believe that the eyebrow can be a sign of a noble character. If you are happy then your eyebrows move with expression and emotion, but if you are suffering they are low and close together.

The ancient Chinese fortune-tellers have distinguished more than thirty distinct eyebrow shapes. Before we examine these in detail we look at general readings that can be made from various types of eyebrow.

We can tell whether a person is a coward or courageous from the shape of the eyebrow. If your eyebrow bone is strong and well formed, then you are courageous and not afraid to stand out in a crowd. You particularly like to concentrate on your studies or hobbies. By nature you are hot-tempered and if you believe you are right you will continue an argument until you have convinced the other party. If a woman has a prominent eyebrow bone she is likely to be lonely and will probably have an unstable relationship with her husband.

If the eyebrow hairs grow upwards this is a sign of courage but people with this kind of eyebrow tend to be violent (Figure 7). Sometimes they upset others by their words and sometimes they harm them by their actions. As a result they will have a bad conscience in old age. If the hairs grow downwards then you are likely to be a coward and cannot maintain a stable or lengthy marriage. If the top part of the eyebrow hair grows downwards and the lower part grows upwards so that the hairs meet in the middle, then you worry and tend to be quite cowardly. The Chinese refer to this hair growth as 'cuddling' hair. Someone with this sort of eyebrow will not live to old age.

Figure 7

If your eyebrow is thick and dark and the hairs grow in different directions, you are likely to suffer bad luck (Figure 8). You will either spend time in prison or have a serious conflict with someone in authority. If you have thin, clear eyebrows which are light in colour, you are unlikely to worry; your mind will be untroubled and you will not be involved in demanding work. You will tend to lead a comfortable lifestyle. If the hairs at the head of the eyebrows sprout upwards in a different direction from the main body, then you are likely to leave home or go abroad at an early age and will probably have a difficult life. If your eyebrow hairs are short and scattered at the eyebrow tail (Figure 9) you probably want to be popular with the opposite sex, whereas if your eyebrow is thick at the eyebrow head and then becomes scattered, you have little willpower and find it extremely hard to forgive others. Eyebrows which are close together but scattered throughout their length are a sign of bad luck, laziness and an inability to take events seriously.

Figure 8

Figure 9

If one of your eyebrows is higher than the other your presumed mother or father are not in fact your real mother or father. Someone whose eyebrows are close together probably finds it difficult to forgive people even if he has been offended by accident. He will also tend to be impatient. A wide gap between the eyebrows indicates a person who is likely to be easygoing and forget wrongs quickly; however, he cannot keep his word and tends to change his mind easily. This type of person follows the crowd and is very bad at managing family affairs. If the hairs on your eyebrow are smooth and growing well but two or three curl against the direction of the others then you are lonely.

If your eyebrow is dull and dry and has the colour of dead wood you are likely to encounter bad luck throughout your life. This sometimes means a short life so it is wise to take care of your health. An eyebrow which is dark and has a matt colour and round eyes indicates someone with a leaning towards theft, even though he may not be short of money. He may well take money or goods just for the thrill of stealing. If your eyebrow has a slight green tinge or a black tinge on the surrounding skin then somebody in the family will have a serious illness. However, if your eyebrow is white and dull in colour, then somebody close to you, perhaps a member of your family or even you yourself, will die soon. A person with an eyebrow which has patchy colours of hair which are glossy and strong is likely to enjoy good health, fulfil promises and will have a successful life.

An eyebrow with a mole which is bright and black is a sign of a good education and a good family background. Such a person is likely to be well thought of by others and respected for his wisdom. If the mole is grey and dull then the opposite applies; in addition one of his family will die by accident. If your eyebrow is scarred or cut then your brothers, sisters and other members of the family will not help each other. You are also likely to have many children.

If one hair grows much longer than the others in a person more than fifty years of age then he is likely to have a long life. Such a hair which grows before the age of fifty is a sign that the person's health is deteriorating. A long hair growing upwards suggests that a man does not get on well with his wife, but a long hair growing downwards over the eyebrow tail indicates that he will have a long life. If the end of this hair is weak or broken, then he does not have a good relationship with his children and the children tend to argue amongst themselves.

P'eng Cho and the Eight Immortals

P'eng Cho spent his days ploughing the paddy fields with his oxen. It was a job he had to do since his father was dead and his mother relied on P'eng Cho, her only son, to support her. One day a wise fortune-teller was passing by and commented how hard the young boy was working. The wise man paused for a moment, then continued, 'I have looked at the five features of your face and read your physiognomy. I have to warn you that you will die on your twentieth birthday.' That evening P'eng Cho told his mother what the fortune-teller had foretold. She was heartbroken to hear this news, but what could she do – the wise man must have given an accurate prediction.

Several years later the Eight Immortals were walking by P'eng Cho's paddy fields and decided to cut across the narrow causeway which divided the watery expanses. For fear of wetting these strangers Peng Cho pulled his oxen to a halt until they had crossed safely. The Immortals were impressed by Peng Cho's kindness and commented on how thoughtful and hard-working he was. On returning home that evening the young boy told his mother how eight unusually dressed people had stopped to speak to him. From his description P'eng Cho's mother immediately realized that they must be the Eight Immortals and told her son to ask them for help if they ever walked by his fields again.

Two days later, the final day of P'eng Cho's life, the Eight Immortals did indeed walk by his paddy fields again. On looking up from his plough, the boy's heart jumped and he and his oxen knelt down in front of the holy people. The Eight Immortals wanted to find out what was troubling the young boy, and so P'eng Cho revealed the fortune-teller's prediction. Finally P'eng Cho lifted his eyes to the Eight Immortals and pleaded, 'If it is within your power to grant me life, please do so.' The holy men and women were impressed with the young boy and promised him long life so he could serve his mother well. Each Immortal gave a gift of 100 years of life to P'eng Cho, then they disappeared. P'eng Cho dropped his hoe in excitement, not realizing that as it fell it killed a poisonous snake. This was the very snake which would have killed P'eng Cho, just as the fortune-teller had predicted.

1-CHARACTER EYEBROW (*Figure 10*)

Figure 10

The hair is thick and the roots can be seen quite clearly. The eyebrow is tail-shaped, straight and round at the end. It should grow beyond the eye tail and looks like the Chinese character for the number 1 (一).

Someone with this eyebrow will come from a large family and is likely to be successful in business at an early age. He is wealthy and respected and will have a long and happy marriage.

8-CHARACTER EYEBROW (*Figure 11*)

Figure 11

The eyebrow is Y-shaped and the hair grows thinly and is scattered at the eyebrow tail. It is called 8-character eyebrow because it looks like the Chinese character for 8 (八).

If you have this type of eyebrow you will be lonely with few friends; even your family does not enjoy living with you. Your marriage will be unhappy and you will have few children. Even if good opportunities come your way you cannot take advantage of them. However, you will never be very poor and will have a long life.

GHOST EYEBROW (*Figure 12*)

Figure 12

The eyebrow is low, curved and short; however, the hairs do not lie with the curve but are straight and grow upwards.

This means you do not have good intentions and have only two thoughts in your heart. One is how to hurt the opposite sex and the other is a desire to steal. As a result you will never be successful in business and will have a short life.

SHARP-KNIFE EYEBROW (*Figure 13*)

Figure 13

This is a dagger-shaped eyebrow with a sharp head, wide tail and rough hair.

The sharp-knife eyebrow signifies a cunning nature; your face may be kind but your heart is hard. Even though you have little success you tend to show off and are boastful. In the end you will fail and suffer a painful death by accident.

ROLLING, CIRCULAR EYEBROW (*Figure 14*)

Figure 14

The hairs are thick, black and curl in the same direction. This eyebrow is rarely seen but tends to occur on the faces of military leaders.

These eyebrows denote a rich, noble and authoritarian person. His relationships with his family are not good.

BROOM EYEBROW (*Figure 15*)

Figure 15

The hairs on the eyebrows head are thick but the hairs on the tail are scattered and sparse so that it has the appearance of a broom.

Although you may have many brothers and sisters you do not maintain close contact with them. The members of your family find it difficult to help one another. Your relationship with your children is difficult and you are likely to have an uncomfortable and impoverished old age.

LITTLE-BROOM EYEBROW (*Figure 16*)

Figure 16

This eyebrow is the same shape as the previous one but does not reach the eyetail. It is considered to be even less lucky than the broom eyebrow.

Someone with a little-broom eyebrow can be cunning, impatient and hot-tempered. You are not on good terms with your brothers and sisters and have a bad relationship with your wife and children. You tend to get in trouble with the law and are not a good judge of business matters.

CLEAR AND BEAUTIFUL EYEBROW (*Figure 17*)

Figure 17

This eyebrow is long and slightly curved. Although there are many hairs their roots cannot be seen. If the eyebrow is short and high, but still has the same hair growth, then the interpretation is the same.

You are trustworthy and can certainly be relied upon to keep your promises. You are willing to reach a compromise should any difficulties arise in your family and so are able to maintain steady relationships. You will be rich and respected all your life.

MORTAL EYEBROW (*Figure 18*)

Figure 18

The hairs on this eyebrow are long, rough and thick and the eyebrow tail grows downwards. The body of the eyebrow is bushy and wide but short.

You are hot-tempered and often lonely. You are very keen on having friends of the opposite sex and tend to get on well with them. You will marry late and even after marriage will maintain this interest in the opposite sex. You will have children late in life, but your family will not readily help you. This shape is considered a poor sign in physiognomy.

SWORD EYEBROW (*Figure 19*)

Figure 19

This grows well above the eye and is straight, long, wide and almost flat. The hairs are thick and grow in the same direction.

The sword eyebrow denote a wise person who has the power to control a large business or organization. You are a born leader and even in unfortunate times have the strength to pull through and succeed. Your life will be long and you are likely to have many children.

RISING EYEBROW (*Figure 20*)

Figure 20

The eyebrow is long and grows evenly beyond the eye tail, rising like a long knife.

You like having your own way and always claim to be in the right; therefore you have the capacity to be dominant and argumentative. You always want to win and often do. Success will come to you early and you will continue to be moderately successful into old age. However, your relationship with your wife/husband is not always stable.

WILLOW-LEAF-SHAPE EYEBROW (*Figure 21*)

Figure 21

The eyebrow hairs are tangled and grow roughly although their roots can still be clearly seen. The eyebrow has a slightly curved shape.

You are very kind and friendly and are honest with your friends. You are also clever and have an aptitude for learning. You enjoy being involved in relationships with the opposite sex. You have the potential to be rich and respected, and will have a powerful friend who helps you. Children will arrive late in life.

NEW MOON EYEBROW (*Figure 22*)

Figure 22

The eyebrow is long, well formed, high above the eye, and the hairs are glossy.

You are very kind and have a large family with whom you are on good terms. You will have a loving wife/husband and children, and as a family will be rich and respected.

BURIAL OR CRYING EYEBROW (*Figure 23*)

Figure 23

The eyebrow head is higher than the tail and the hairs grow downwards, scattering in all directions. The eyebrow does not grow beyond the eye tail.

You are very selfish, cunning, and adept at pretending to be kind while wondering in your heart how you can cheat others. You will be fairly wealthy but this does not mean you will be respected. This eyebrow should be compared with the eye to see if it also gives a similar reading.

DRAGON EYEBROW (*Figure 24*)

Figure 24

The eyebrow head rises straight up and then slopes down. The hair is dark and bright and the eyebrow generally has a good appearance.

If you have this type of eyebrow, you are very clever and have a good head for business; you have a courageous nature. You are likely to be very rich and respected and probably come from a large family.

SILKWORM EYEBROW (*Figure 25*)

Figure 25

The body of the eyebrow is curled and the eyebrow itself rises upwards. It has a smooth shape and a bright colour.

This is the eyebrow of a person who is clever, wise and trusted. You probably have a clerical job or work in a disciplined field. During your life you have the opportunity to be rich and noble.

LION-SHAPED EYEBROW (*Figure 26*)

Figure 26

The eyebrow curls and its body is wide and curved. Although it is thick the roots can be clearly seen. The shape resembles a lion lying down.

Your eyebrow has an angry shape but you are kind by nature. You either have a clerical job or work in a disciplined field. You are rich and respected and will have a long life. Unfortunately you probably have a bad relationship with your wife/husband and children and are often involved in family quarrels.

LONG-LIFE EYEBROW (*Figure 27*)

Figure 27

The body of the eyebrow is wide and the hairs are longer at the eyebrow tail than at the eyebrow head. They are dark in colour and have a glossy sheen. The eyebrow head curves slightly downwards.

You will have a long life and be famous as a writer. You have the opportunity to be very rich. You are naturally kind and friendly and enjoy the company of the opposite sex.

There are obviously variations in these types of eyebrow. Some eyebrows are a combination of different shapes so care should be taken when reading the owner's character. In addition to distinguishing various types of eyebrow, it is also necessary to have a basic understanding of eyebrow shapes and hair growth.

LONG EYEBROW (*Figure 28*)

Figure 28

The hairs grow in the same direction and have a bright, glossy appearance.

You are likely to have a high IQ and be gifted in intellectual debate. You probably have a large family and maintain good relationships not only with your family but with your friends. However, if you have this type of eyebrow but your other features are unbalanced, the above reading will not apply. If your features are well balanced and you have a long eyebrow you will be lucky, especially in middle age.

SHORT EYEBROW (*Figure 29*)

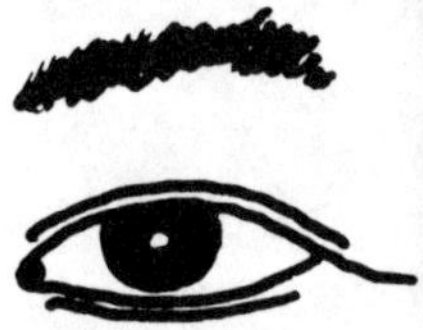
Figure 29

The hairs on the eyebrow are rough and uneven in length. The eyebrow itself is shorter than the eye.

You come from a small family and will probably have a short life. You are not on particularly good terms with your family and have difficulty in maintaining long relationships. You will also be unfortunate in your business affairs.

BIG EYEBROW (*Figure 30*)

This eyebrow is long, wide and well formed.

Figure 30

Someone who is courageous and not afraid to face people or speak his mind will have this type of eyebrow. A woman with such an eyebrow will be more dominant than her husband, who is likely to have a short, thin eyebrow and enjoys working at home and helping her in domestic duties.

5
The Five Features: The Eyes

The eyes are the most important feature of the face because they have the power to control the other four features. When we look at somebody we usually notice the eyes first. Eyes that are bright, clear and well formed suggest that the owner is happy and fairly fortunate; even if the other features are out of balance, the eye can help improve them. Chinese fortune-tellers have distinguished many distinct eye shapes which we examine individually later in this chapter. The readings do not mention different eye colourings since physiognomy originally applied to the Chinese people whose eyes are usually brown in colour. The character is, therefore, interpreted according to the shape and clarity of the eye itself.

The eye is particularly useful in physiognomy – the other features of the face tend to alter over the years whereas the eye remains a constant feature, enabling us to give a fairly accurate reading. An example of a well-shaped eye for a woman is the almond shape, which signifies long life (Figure 31). The iris should fill a large area of the eye and the colour should be distinct. In addition, the face should be bright and alert. The eye should not protrude outwards or look angry. The white of the eye should not be bloodshot. The pupil should always be clear and bright. A well-shaped eye can be marred if the pupil is dull or the eyebrow is too low. The Chinese say that the low eyebrow is like a black cloud which covers the moon. Someone with this type of eye makes many plans but always has difficulty in carrying them out. People with large eyes are not cowardly and are likely to be successful in business; they also have many friends of the

Figure 31

opposite sex. Dull, protruding eyes or round and staring eyes are not considered good. They belong to an unsuccessful person who will never be famous. His life will be plagued with bad luck and he will not live to old age. A woman who has round, protruding eyes will have an unstable marital relationship. Sparkling eyes which do not protrude mean that the owner will be respected even though he may not be rich. Someone whose eyes protrude and have a staring glare will probably die by accident; however, if the eye has a black tinge the person is probably very clever and talented in a creative field. Eyes that are small, round, sluggish and dull indicate a foolish person. A constant gaze means an honest, reliable person who will listen to the opinions of others. Such people do not want to cause trouble and are so honest that they do not worry about being cheated by others.

Someone whose eyes always appear to be searching and darting to and fro is cunning and plans dark secrets. A person whose eyes remain on the same level, not darting upwards or downwards, whether he is walking or sitting, is judged to be honest and kind. A person whose eyes look upwards while he is speaking has a tendency to show off and is usually arrogant. Somebody who always looks down, even when speaking, is likely to be dangerous and cunning. This is different from a person who looks down with a fixed gaze; he may well be thinking about something. However, even though this is not bad, he still cannot be described as wise or noble. If the face remains level but the eyes move from the left to the right, then that person may be planning evil, which could be directed towards you or your family. (This does not apply to a cross-eyed person or those born with a squint or deformity.) Anybody with darting eyes who has an angry look is thinking evil. It is best to avoid such people since they cannot form close friendships. Someone whose eyes slowly wander around probably has a good business head but is prone to lie and cannot be trusted too deeply. A person who sometimes closes his eyes or looks down before speaking may die by accident; his body may not be found and as a result he will have no burial. Someone with one eye larger than the other probably has a different father or mother from the one he thinks he has; he is perhaps adopted. Should a man's left eye be smaller than his right he is likely to be scared of his wife. If his right eye is smaller than his left then the opposite applies: he is probably rude to his wife and quarrelsome with his family. A woman whose left eye is smaller than her right will have to work hard to support her husband since he probably suffers from weak health or is unemployed. If her right eye is smaller than her left then her husband will have difficulty supporting her and they will frequently quarrel.

A person who has no fold on his eyelid is likely to react very strongly to emotional situations (Figure 32). A person over forty years of age with many lines at the outside corner of the eye (fishtails or crow's feet) is capable of sorting out problems. If somebody under the age of forty has these lines it means that he pretends to be hard working but in fact does very little; however, it is difficult to prove this. A young man who has many fishtail wrinkles at the outer corner of the eye is likely to have more than one wife. If he only has one wife, this could also mean that he will die by accident. The Chinese consider this to be an inauspicious sign. It is normal to have three or four fishtail wrinkles; more than four is considered to be above average for a young man. A man whose fishtail wrinkles grow upwards will be successful in everything he does and will also have a strong love for his wife. But if his fishtail wrinkles grow downwards his business is not going well; he will suffer bad luck and will probably end up divorcing his wife. Fishtail wrinkles that are like scissors, with one running upwards and the other crossing it downwards, indicates a person who will not accept the advice of his family. He is never particularly happy in his work and tends to grumble frequently. As a result of this he is often lonely.

Figure 32

Eyes which look watery but beautiful are considered to denote a lascivious nature. Someone with worried eyes is having a difficult time coping with his problems; although he works hard he never seems to gain success. Clear eyes are a sign that good fortune lies ahead. Somebody with muddy eyes (that is, eyes whose colour is not distinct) or searching eyes will never be wealthy. If the white of the eye covers a large area and the iris is small accidents are likely to befall this person. It is certainly not a good idea to form business partnerships with the owner of such eyes. Green veins underneath the eyes mean there is likely to be a disaster in the near future; if the person sleeps with his eyes half open he will probably die by accident. Someone whose eyes are bloodshot through the iris or who has bloodshot veins reaching the iris must take care since he will have an accident in the near future. Bloodshot veins which go through the iris and reach the pupil are a sign of death in the near future. The two exceptions to this rule are the bloodshot eyes that result from too much drink or from sickness.

Position of Iris

TOP THREE WHITE (*Figure 33*)

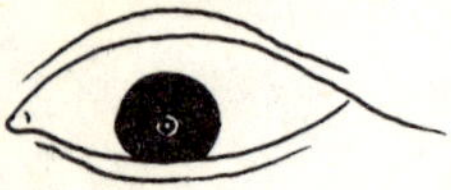

Figure 33

The iris is at the bottom of the eye and there is white on three sides.

You have a strong mind and a hot temper and tend to look down on other people. Even when speaking to others you can be cruel and upset people easily without realizing. You are not renowned for your tact. Your business ventures are likely to fail and you have a bad relationship with your family. You are unlikely to have many friends.

BOTTOM THREE WHITE (*Figure 34*)

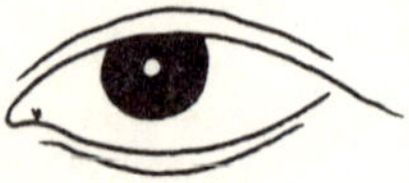

Figure 34

The iris is in the upper part of the eye and there are three areas of white, one on each side and one beneath the iris.

This type of eye belongs to a cruel, hard person. He rarely considers the feelings of other people and schemes like a tiger or a wolf. Money will not come easily to him even though he works hard: he is capable of causing a great deal of trouble and accidents. His relations with his family are also troubled. If a woman has bottom three white she is in danger of harming her husband violently or will suffer a divorce. She may also have problems during pregnancy.

FOUR WHITE (*Figure 35*)

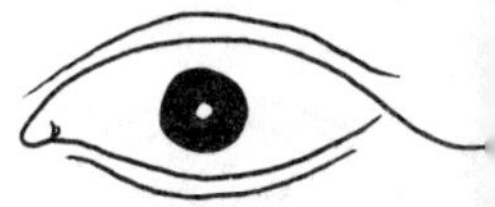
Figure 35

The iris is in the middle of the eye and is surrounded by the four white areas.

Whether this eye belongs to a man or a woman they are scheming and hot-tempered. They are lascivious by nature and even if rich and respected will have an unfortunate old age.

Types of Eye

TRIANGULAR EYES (*Figure 36*)

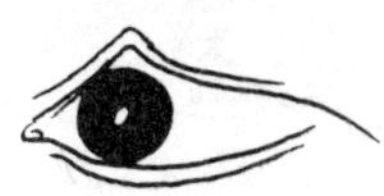
Figure 36

The iris and the white have distinct colours and the eyes are alert. This type of eye is usually accompanied by a strong eyebrow.

If you have this combination then you will be rich, respected and successsful in youth. You very much like to win and have a mind that is not easily changed. Your heart, however, is cunning and dangerous and you often quarrel with your wife/husband and family. The chances are that your old age will be unhappy and unfortunate. A man whose iris and white of the eye are muddy with fishtail wrinkles growing downwards is probably scheming and cruel. Even if he has a small amount of money he will spend it on enjoyment and has a tendency to waste his savings. He will treat his friends dishonestly and always try to find a way of cheating people. If a woman has these eyes she is likely to have a bad relationship with her husband and will secretly take another lover.

WHEEL EYES (*Figure 37*)

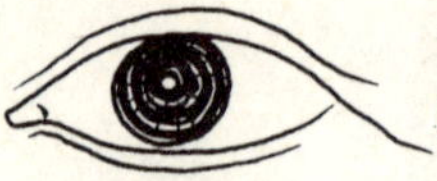

Figure 37

These eyes have coloured lines in the iris and are known as angry eyes.

Such eyes are likely to belong to a violent person who will die by accident. Someone with these eyes will have a bad relationship with his wife and tend not to have children. He will by no means be a good friend.

FIRE-WHEEL EYES (*Figure 38*)

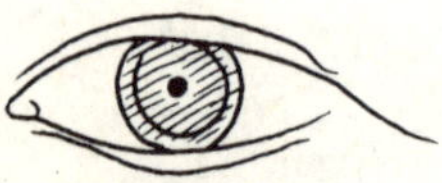

Figure 38

The edge of the iris has a red or light green or blue ring. Sometimes the centre of the eye has another, lighter-coloured ring.

This person is hot-tempered, angry and capable of killing. It is possible that he will commit suicide or meet death by accident.

SAND EYES (*Figure 39*)

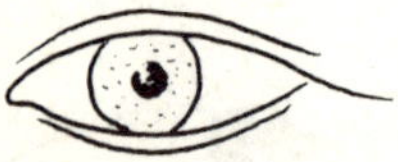

Figure 39

These eyes have flecks of colour in the iris. Although they look angry they are not cruel.

You are likely to quarrel with your family and your relations and will probably have bad luck during your life.

MOLE EYES (*Figure 40*)

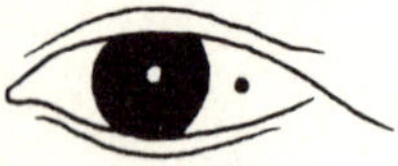

Figure 40

This eye has a fleck of colour in the white of the eye; this is a bad sign even if the eye has a good shape.

Someone with this type of eye is unlucky and is likely to squander any money that he may have received from an inheritance. In the end he will lose everything he owns.

DRUNK EYES (*Figure 41*)

Figure 41

The eyes are bloodshot. The iris slopes downwards and has a sleepy look. The whites of the eye tend to have a yellow tinge and the fishtail has many short wrinkles.

This is not a good eye for a man or a woman since it denotes a lascivious nature. A person with such eyes is considered to be unlucky in life.

UNWRINKLED EYES (*Figure 42*)

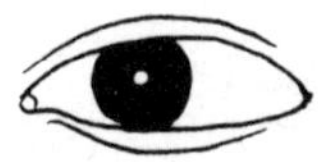

Figure 42

This eye tends to have no wrinkles even after the age of forty and the eye tail is rounded.

This eye belongs to a genius or to somebody who is very intelligent. He is capable of making you believe anything and has very strong powers of persuasion. He will probably have trouble in his relationships and always end up in difficulty.

PEA-BLOSSOM EYES (*Figure 43*)

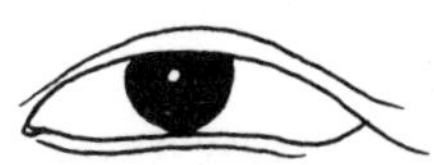

Figure 43

The eyes are long and bow-shaped. The iris and the white are not clear.

You tend to observe people from the side of your eyes rather than gazing straight at them. Your main preoccupation is to make an impression upon the opposite sex. You are, however, quite capable of having successful relationships. You are also quite gifted and successful in the arts.

ELEPHANT EYES (*Figure 44*)

Figure 44

There are wrinkles above and below the eye. The eye itself is narrow and long.

People with these eyes are generally popular and noted for their kindness, friendliness and wisdom. They have a creative nature. If this eye is matched with longevity eyebrows (see p. 53) then the owner is fortunate and will have a long life.

LION EYES (*Figure 45*)

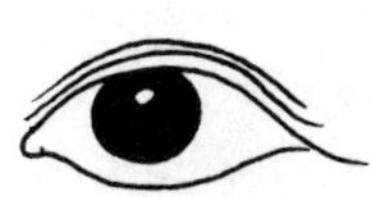

Figure 45

These eyes are large and the iris and the white are clear. The iris is at the top of the eye and there are lines on the lid. This eye has a beautiful shape.

If you have this type of eye you are respected and usually work in a high-ranking job. Most eyes are thought to be unlucky if they have a thick eyebrow but these are the exception. Provided they do not slant downwards, you will be lucky and have a long life.

TIGER EYES (*Figure 46*)

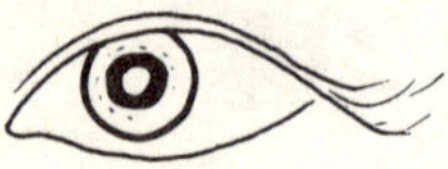

Figure 46

The iris is golden-coloured and the eyes gaze straight ahead. They have a line on the eyelid but none underneath and the fishtails are short and scattered with no particular direction.

If you are in the company of somebody with such eyes you will notice that everybody behaves sensibly. People usually respond to such a person by answering his questions, while looking straight at him. This person, although rich, does not enjoy his money. He is not particularly lucky and is quite often lonely. His life will also be difficult and he will probably die by accident.

OXEN EYES (*Figure 47*)

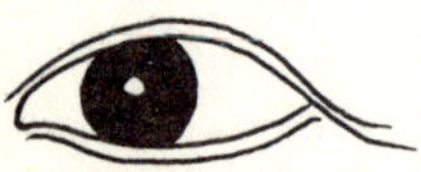

Figure 47

These eyes are large but not protruding. The white and the iris have very clear colours.

Such eyes belong to a fairly relaxed, gentle person who does not have strong emotional reactions. If there are long wrinkles above and below the eye and the fishtail wrinkles rise upwards then the person is trustworthy and can be relied upon to keep his promises. He is usually well dressed and will live a long life.

PIG EYES (*Figure 48*)

Figure 48

The iris is black and not particularly clear. The white of the eye and the skin on the lid is thick and heavy.

You tend to be hot-tempered and cruel. Even if you have money you can never enjoy it; you will usually die by accident. If you have little money then you will not meet an accident but will have a difficult life. You are unlikely to have children.

MONKEY EYES (*Figure 49*)

These eyes are short in length and the iris is positioned towards the upper lid. The iris is dark with a yellow tinge and the upper line above the eye is rounded and steeply sloping towards the eye corner and beyond. This person blinks frequently and tends to look down.

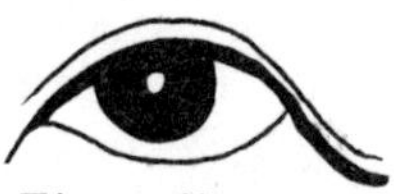
Figure 49

By nature you are lively, alert and courageous. You are particularly good at making plans and are well respected by others. Although you will have difficult times in your life you are usually quite fortunate. You have a monkey's nature and are particularly fond of eating fruit.

CRANE EYES (*Figure 50*)

The eyes are large and the iris is round and clear and placed in the centre of the eye. There will usually be more than two wrinkles on the upper lid and the eyes themselves are long and beautifully shaped.

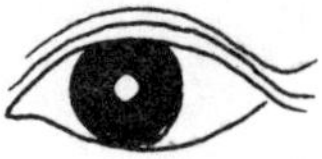
Figure 50

You have an honest face and an aptitude to forgive people. You not only make friends easily but are able to keep them. Throughout your life you will be rich and respected.

EGRET EYES (*Figure 51*)

These are long in shape with slight yellow tinges in the iris or in the white of the eye. The iris is sometimes positioned high in the eye and the upper wrinkle is long. There is no lower line.

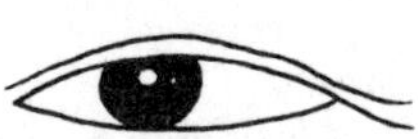
Figure 51

This eye belongs to a lonely person who will suffer bad luck. Although he has close family and friends they never seem able to help him. Even though he may be rich he will finally loose everything.

WILD-GOOSE EYES (*Figure 52*)

Figure 52

These eyes have a large black pupil and the iris has a golden tinge. There are upper wrinkle and lower wrinkles and the eye is long and well defined in shape.

You have a relaxed character and a lively nature and are particularly good at making friends. You probably have an average position at work but are satisfied with your status. By nature you are honest and have the potential to be rich. Your relationship with your family is good.

SWALLOW EYES (*Figure 53*)

Figure 53

These eyes are deep set with a long line above and below. The eyes themselves are clear and bright.

You have a comfortable life, are usually well dressed and keep promises faithfully. You will probably have children late in life but will be unfortunate in them since you will not be able to rely on them.

HORSE EYES (*Figure 54*)

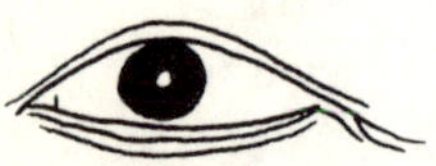

Figure 54

The upper lid is soft and the lower lid has several folds of skin; the fishtail wrinkles grow downwards. The eye itself is slightly bulging and watery.

You will have a difficult life; even though you work hard you will have little success. If you are also thin and your facial skin is taut you will have a bad relationship with your family and will be extremely unlucky in whatever you attempt to do.

LAMB EYES (*Figure 55*)

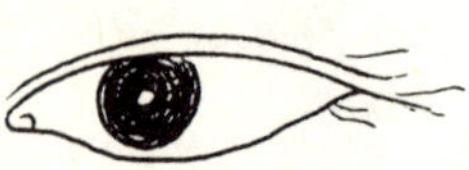

Figure 55

The eyes have a dark cast and the iris has a yellow tinge; sometimes it is possible to see wheel-shaped lines in the iris. The upper lid has a fold but the lower lid does not. The skin beneath the eye is flat, thin and unlined. The fishtail wrinkles are scattered.

These eyes are associated with an unfortunate person; even if he is wealthy he will never get a chance to enjoy his fortune. He will probably have a poor, lonely life and die by accident.

We have listed above the basic shapes of the eye, although you will often see variations on these shapes. Before carrying out detailed reading of the eye, it is possible to make a judgement based on first impressions. A good eye should look bright, alert and wide. It should be judged in relation to the other features.

6
The Five Features: The Nose

The Nose in Relation to the Cheekbones

The Chinese say that it is impossible to do predictions using the nose without also taking into account the shape of the cheekbones. The nose is like an emperor and the cheekbones stand on either side like two guards in the Imperial Court. They are thought of as three mountains which sit in a straight line; the other two mountains of the face are the chin and the forehead. The nose is the central mountain, the left cheek the eastern mountain, the right cheek the western mountain, the forehead the southern mountain (Chinese maps traditionally place south at the top) and the chin the northern mountain. The nose is the most important and controls the other four. Since the cheekbones are the guards or the protectors they should bend towards the nose. If either side is weak then the central mountain has no assistance in controlling destiny. The other two mountains, that is the forehead and the chin, are not as important as the cheekbones. If the left cheekbone is higher than the right, the nose is not in control; this person is not capable of carrying off any bold venture. If the cheekbones are well formed but the nose is weak, the overall prediction will be inauspicious. If the nose is well formed but the cheekbones are weak, the prediction will also be unlucky. If the balance looks harmonious then we can give a good reading. The ancient fortune-tellers say, 'A flower is beautiful and needs green leaves to match it.'

As with most areas of physiognomy, the nose and cheekbones need to match in order to give a proper reading. If you see someone with a broad face, prominent cheekbones and a small nose then you cannot give a good reading. The opposite can apply – the nose may be large but the cheekbones and the face are narrow. In this case we would predict bad luck at some stage of life. Someone with prominent cheekbones but a small, flat nose has no power over his subordinates since no one is willing to obey his orders.

The best cheekbones should be rounded but not obvious. High cheekbones are luckier than low ones and in general they ought to be smooth and round, without any bumps or lumps. It is important to note that a high cheekbone is judged in relation to the front part of the cheek but ought to be matched to line A shown in Figure 56. A cheekbone which follows this line is considered to be very lucky; the person concerned is always planning for the future, refuses to give up and will always be successful. If

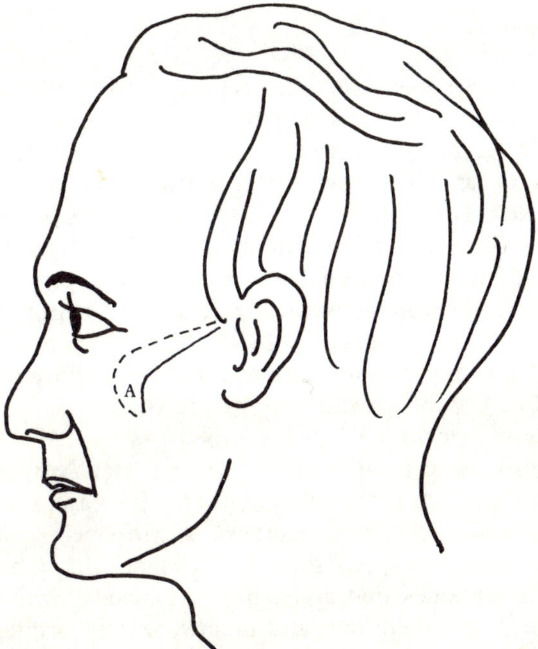

Figure 56

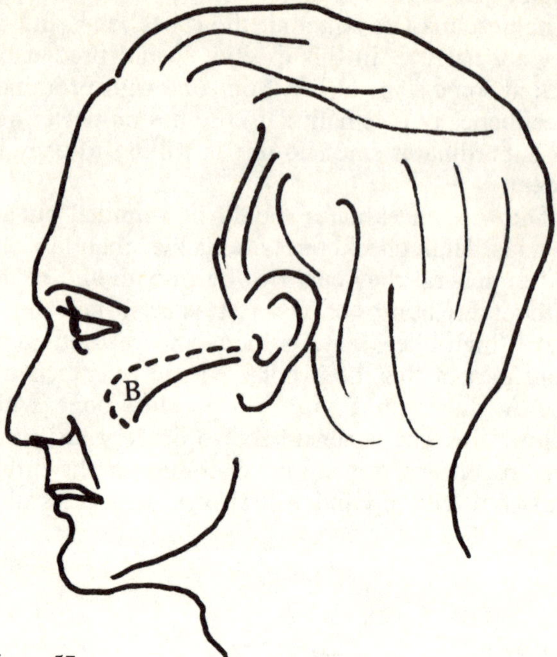

Figure 57

the cheekbones follow line B (Figure 57) the reading will not be particularly good.

If the line of the cheekbone protrudes and the skin is taut 'as a drum skin', this means an unlucky and unsuccessful life. Such a person will be lazy and care very little about his actions. When he comes by a small amount of money he will become arrogant and find it difficult to form any close friendships. If a woman has these features she will have an unstable relationship with her husband and her children; she is likely to be separated or divorced.

Someone whose cheekbone is flat or dented or has been broken in an accident will not want responsibility and is usually unambitious. By nature he is not power-seeking or courageous. Most people with these features spend their lives in labouring jobs.

Cheekbones that are high and obvious, with the skin below them taut and hollow, are, according to Chinese physiognomy, a sign of drug addiction.

Above we have given a basic knowledge of the cheekbones; now we examine in greater detail the shape and colour of the nose.

The Nose

In the Five Elements the nose is linked to earth. It is also the middle mountain of the face and controls the other four mountains. By examining the nose we can discover whether someone has a pure heart and mind, whether he is trustworthy or cunning. It is important that the nose is in harmony with the other features; as commander of the face it should be well supported by the other four features.

The nose should not be too thin, nor should it be upturned. If you look at someone straight on you should not be able to see the nostrils too clearly. The left nostril is called *lan t'ai* and the right is known as *t'ing wei*; together they are referred to as *lan t'ing* (Figure 58). The *lan t'ing* (both nostrils) on the well-balanced nose ought to be the same size. We can sense simply by looking at a nose whether it is strongly built and if the air passageways are clear.

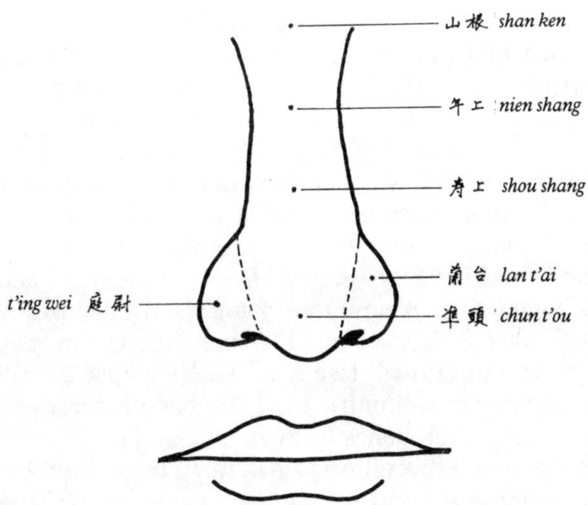

Figure 58 The Positions of the Nose

The skin should be bright and clear; the tip of the nose should be rounded and muscular and not look too narrow.

The ancient Chinese divided the nose into four more areas (Figure 58): the *shan ken*, the *nien shang*, the *shou shang* and the *chun t'ou*. The *shan ken* is at the top, the *nien shang* and the *shou shang* are in the middle, and the *chun t'ou* is the tip. If your *nien shang* and the *shou shang* are rounded, and the other features are in harmony, you will have a long life. If the tip of the nose is also round you will have the opportunity to become rich; you will never be very poor. Someone whose nose tip is too round, with wide nostrils and a lump on the end, has a lascivious nature. Somebody whose nose tip and nostrils are large and thick will be rich and noble. If the tip of the nose is thin and pointed he will be poor and lonely. A nose that is pointed and slightly bent indicates a poisonous heart; such a person is only concerned in harming others and if possible deriving some benefit from his cunning ways.

A long nose is more desirable than a short one, but we must always remember to examine the proportions in relation to the rest of the face. A large face with a small nose is considered to be a sign of bad luck. If the nose is straight, well formed, and the bone of the nose is not obvious, then we can predict that this person is decisive, determined and fortunate in life. He is patient in unfavourable circumstances and has the strength and persistence to continue until difficulties are resolved.

Someone with large cheekbones and a small nose will have a difficult life; he is likely to have little money and an unstable relationship with his wife and children. By nature he is dishonest and dishonourable. A nose that is high and thin, with a blade that feels soft, is a bad sign; the owner may have wealth but will lose it easily. By nature he will be argumentative, unfriendly, and has a tendency to show off. Weak bones in the nose are considered to be a sign of a short life and bad luck, but a nose that is strong and straight is a sign of a decisive and successful businessman. If the bone of the nose is obvious it is an indication that the person will not accept good advice. He will also come across difficult problems but will give up easily without a fight.

If the nose feels soft and fleshy, the heart is also soft; this is the nose of a person who is very sympathetic to others, particularly when they need help. This person will never be very successful since he is too soft-hearted; it is not in his nature to be calculating, and so he finds himself easily cheated by cunning people.

The ancient Chinese fortune-tellers say that a man with a nose like an eagle's beak will peck at another man's heart; by nature he is selfish and dangerous. Sometimes you may see someone who appears to have a rounded tip to his nose but on close examination you will notice that the nose really has a sharp point; in this case you must be careful not to fall into the traps he sets, because he is like a wolf in sheep's clothing.

If a man's nose is slightly bent to the left, his father will die before his mother; if it is slightly bent to the right, his mother will die before his father. The opposite rule applies for women. A nose that is very crooked, with one nostril higher than the other, is a sign that the person's mind is full of evil thoughts even though he may never actually harm anyone (Figure 59). He has a selfish, dishonest nature and will readily use his friends and then desert them. A man whose nose is bent but whose other features are well formed will have the opportunity to be rich, but by the end of his life will lose everything.

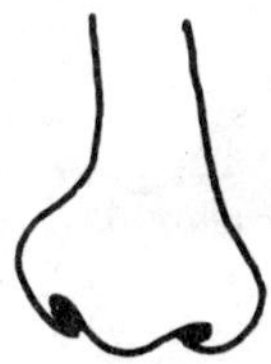

Figure 59

Someone whose nose is thin and dark red in colour will be poor and have no family. He will spend his life trying to pay back the money which he has borrowed. A bump on the *nien shang* or *shou shang* is a sign that the person is neither respected nor well liked; he has a tendency to be unpredictable in behaviour and so finds making friendships very difficult. A nose which is bent at two or three points means that the person may work hard but earn little. He is also prone to disasters, accidents and illness. His middle age will be the most dangerous period of his life.

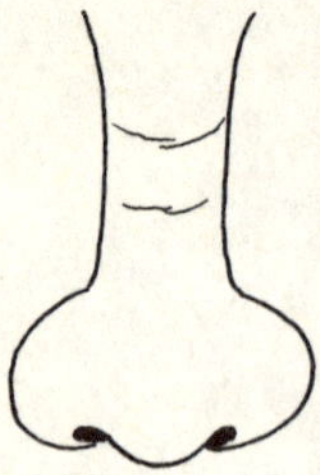

Figure 60

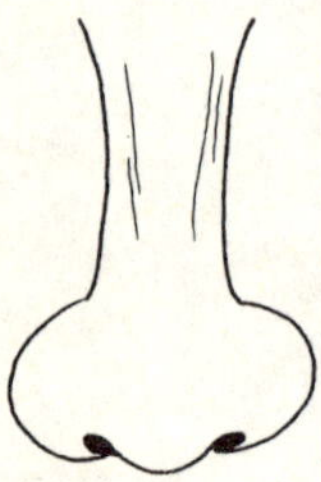

Figure 61

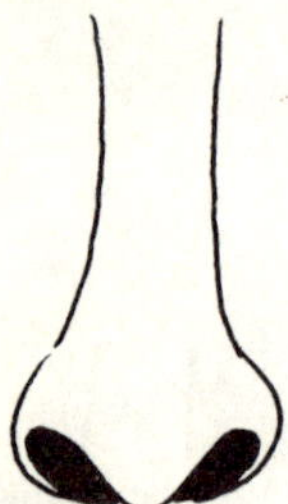

Figure 62

Broken or crossing wrinkles in the *nien shang* or *shou shang* signify a bad accident during some period in life (Figure 60): it is most likely to happen when he is travelling by car, train, plane or horse. If a woman has crossing wrinkles in these two areas, she will go through a dangerous period in childbirth. Someone with vertical lines or wrinkles on the *nien shang* or *shou shang* will have no child of his or her own but is likely to adopt a baby (Figure 61).

Someone whose nostrils are clearly visible from the front will never know real poverty, but will have difficulty saving money, spending it as soon as it arrives. If your *shan ken* or *nien shang* is thin and the nostrils can be clearly seen, you will die in a foreign country, but if the nostrils are not too obvious a more auspicious forecast can be given.

A nose of average size with large nostrils signifies loss of money through gambling (Figure 62). If the holes are rectangular (lengthwise), you will not listen to good advice and therefore lose money easily. If your nostrils are rectangular (widthwise), you are satisfied with your present job but will have difficulty saving money. Triangular holes denote a miserly, greedy nature. Finally, oval-shaped holes (8-character shaped) signify someone who can spend easily or save easily: he never gambles and always has something to show for his earnings.

A well-shaped, rounded nostril signifies a decisive, systematic nature. Such a person is a perfectionist who also likes to arrange the lives of others, but his downfall is that he is selfish and cannot care about his friends. An opposite reading will be given for a small, flat, weak nose. The owner cares for others, but is too kind-hearted to succeed in business.

If the tip of the nose is bright and the skin clear, you will not be wealthy but will have good health, whereas a dark red nose tip signifies a difficult, unhappy life.

A nose which looks burned is referred to by the Chinese as a room on fire. This person will never be successful and is likely to die by accident. A nose which has a normal grey colour belongs to someone who is full of plans and ideas. He will scheme in the face of difficulties and sometimes will be successful. If grey or black tinges suddenly appear on the nose, then take care in the near future since your health may be in danger. Permanent dark marks denote hard work but no gain.

A woman's nose is an indication of the success of her marriage. If her nose is an average size, not too thin, well rounded, glossy, not too hard, and if the nose bone cannot be seen clearly then she will have a good husband. He may not be handsome but he will be kind to her. He will be the sort of man who worries over domestic finances and will do everything he can to support her. Sometimes the five features appear to be balanced and well proportioned but the face is not particularly handsome. However, this is still a good sign since it indicates a happy marriage and good family. Unhappiness in marriage is signified by a face which at first glance appears beautiful but on close inspection reveals a bad feature – for example, a man with a flat nose is likely to quarrel with his wife.

SWORD NOSE (*Figure 63*)

This nose is large and high on the face and the bridge of the nose is sharp and hard to the touch.

You have a bad relationship with your wife/husband and children, and you are also on unfriendly terms with your brothers and sisters. You are not successful at work, home or socially. It is likely that you will die in a foreign country.

Figure 63

LONELY-MOUNTAIN NOSE (*Figure 64*)

The end of the nose is very high. The *nien shou* (two middle positions of the nose combined) are flat and the cheekbones are usually very flat.

You have a good deal of experience but will never be successful, although there are times when you are satisfied and content. In general your life will be difficult and your family will be unable to help. In the end you will have to be self-reliant.

Figure 64

HAIRY NOSE (*Figure 65*)

Figure 65

The most notable features of this nose are the large, hairy nostrils. Although the bridge of the nose looks strong, the tip of the nose is quite thin and flat.

This is the nose of a competitive person. Even if he wins a large amount of money he will soon lose it through gambling; as the Chinese say, 'Left hand in, right hand out.' He will have a difficult life but he is courageous and will try hard to succeed where he has seen others fail. He will be successful in many things but will lose them in the end. Even if he has saved money he has the capacity to lose it quickly, since he takes too many risks.

BUN-BRIDGE NOSE (*Figure 66*)

Figure 66

The *nien shou* protrudes and even though the nose looks big it is quite thin and lacks muscle.

Although you can be humorous and honest you are lonely and have few friends since your behaviour is sometimes erratic. Most of the time your work is not running too smoothly. A woman with a bun-bridge nose will marry twice but will not get on well with her children.

THREE-BENDS NOSE (*Figure 67*)

Figure 67

The *shan ken* is dented and the *nien shou* protrudes. The tip of the nose is sharp and thin.

The three-bends nose is unlucky in physiognomy since it belongs to someone who will be plagued by bad luck all his life. He will never be rich, will have few children and is likely to be divorced or separated early in life.

COLLAPSED (FLAT) NOSE (*Figure 68*)

This nose is very soft and weak, the bridge is flat and the tip of the nose small. Since this nose lacks muscle it does not have the rounded appearance of an average nose. If you look at this person straight on you will be able to see the nostrils very clearly.

Figure 68

A man with a collapsed nose is cowardly, greedy and canny. He is rarely successful and will probably be poor for most of his life. He would like to steal to augment his earnings but does not have the courage. This man will have a short life.

EAGLE-BEAK NOSE (*Figure 69*)

Figure 69

The nose is thin, the *nien shou* protrudes, and the tip of the nose is quite sharp and hooked.

The Chinese say that someone with this nose has 'a poisonous heart'. By nature he is cruel and selfish. He wants to take advantage of others and is quite prepared to endanger himself in the process. Sometimes good opportunities come his way but they quickly disappear. He usually has wholesome relationships, not only with his wife and children but also with his relatives.

KNOT NOSE (*Figure 70*)

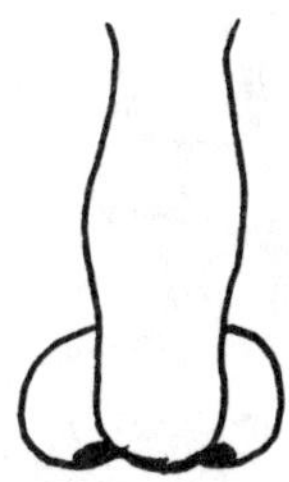
Figure 70

This nose has a rounded lump on the *nien shou* and looks like a knotted rope.

You have a strong will and find it difficult to accept anyone's advice. If you encounter difficulties in the midst of a task, you give up in disgust. You can, however, be good hearted and work very hard but you get little in return. In general the knot nose is considered a poor shape in Chinese physiognomy – poor, that is, in terms of wealth. If a woman has this nose she will live alone after middle age.

PROTRUDING-NOSTRIL NOSE (*Figure 71*)

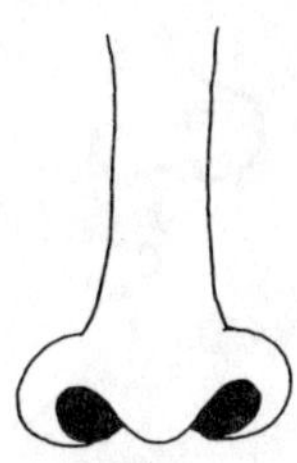
Figure 71

This nose is large and the tip rounded and slightly upturned. It is almost possible to see the complete nostril.

You have great difficulty saving money, and although you are not poor you are incapable of putting savings in a bank. Your money is wasted on frivolous things and you will never be lucky if you gamble. However, your attitude towards money is likely to be 'easy come, easy go'.

NOT-BALANCED NOSE (*Figure 72*)

Figure 72

The main feature of this nose is the unbalanced *lan t'ing* (two sides combined), with one side lower than the other. The reading will be improved if the nose is quite large, the tip of the nose rounded and the bridge straight.

If the nose does not have these additional features then you will quickly lose all your property, particularly any left by inheritance. During periods of difficulty nobody will be able to help you and between the ages of forty-six and forty-seven you will be involved in a disaster.

SAGE'S SON NOSE (Rich and Noble Nose) (*Figure 73*)

Figure 73

The *shan ken* is wide and straight and the line of the nose is strong and well formed. The *nien shang* is long and continues in a straight line to the forehead (*yin t'ang*). The *lan t'ang* are well balanced and the skin is clear and bright.

You do not have preferences and approach all people equally. You will never support the strong against the weak. Throughout life you are likely to be rich and respected and will suffer very few accidents. In general you have a good family and many children.

LAMB NOSE (*Figure 74*)

Figure 74

The tip of the nose is bulbous and the *lan t'ing* are easily distinguished. The *shan ken* is very strong and the *nien shou* is rounded.

You are well known, respected, wealthy, and very successful in your profession, but you are selfish and unkind to both your partner and your children.

DEER NOSE (*Figure 75*)

Figure 75

The tip of the nose is round and the nose generally has a good appearance. The *shan ken* and the *nien shang* are slightly indented but they are nevertheless strong and well formed.

You are kind by nature and can be relied upon to keep your promise, even if you have only known someone for a short time. You will have wealth, long life and a large family.

7
The Five Features: The Mouth

The mouth is not only the means by which we drink, eat and speak, but is also an indication of a kind or a cruel nature. An examination of the mouth will reveal whether a person will speak ill of others or whether his thoughts are always kind. The shape of the mouth and the teeth also provides information about someone's fortune and health. The slightly rounded corners at the ends of the mouth are known as sea corners or *ling* (Figure 76).

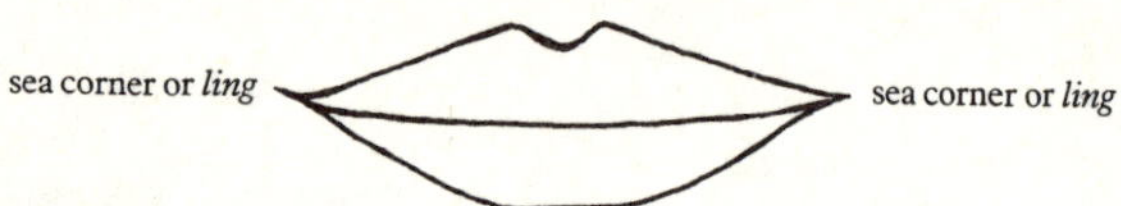

Figure 76

A good mouth is well proportioned with slightly upturned corners; the lips should be quite large and red in colour. A good prediction for marriage, health and career will be given if all the above features are present.

A small mouth should never be combined with a large face; it is considered better to have a large mouth than a small one. A bad reading will be made if the mouth is large but is lacking sea corners or if the lines of the lips are uneven. Uneven lips which have no sea corners signify someone with a cutting tongue who speaks ill of others. He will quickly lose any opportunity to earn a great deal of money. Lips which purse together when the mouth is naturally closed denote a poor person who is little respected. He works hard to please his superiors but has a dishonest nature. The Chinese refer to him as a 'little man'. The owner of lips which are fat, large, bright, glossy and well balanced usually has a healthy body and a strong stomach for eating and drinking. He is wealthy and enjoys good relationships with women.

A bow-shaped mouth which appears to be slightly smiling is a sign of culture and a love of film, art and theatre (Figure 77). Someone with a bow-shaped mouth does not take a great interest in material acquisitions. He will easily make friends with women and has no difficulty in maintaining sensitive friendships. He does not worry about money but will never be poor. A large, wide mouth and a strongly built body signify someone who grasps at opportunities and is always determined to get what he wants regardless of who stands in his way; sometimes he is successful and sometimes he fails. In general his life is very busy and he has few peaceful moments.

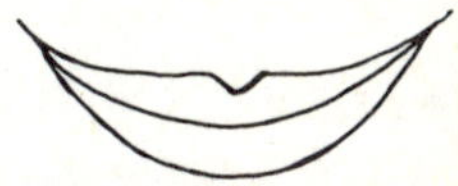

Figure 77

A well-shaped mouth will speak kindly of others, but an ugly-shaped mouth causes much upset. If someone's lips move before he speaks then the Chinese say that 'the heart is not good'. A mouth which is always closed when the person is not speaking is a sign of a strong mind and firm concentration. But if the mouth is always slightly open the owner has a weak mind and will always follow the ideas of others. He is usually lazy in his career and has difficulty finishing any project.

If the bottom part of the upper lip covers the lower lip in the centre of the mouth, you are determined that others should follow your ideas or decisions, since you think you are always right. The Chinese say that the standard mouth for a man ought to be one in which the upper lip is slightly larger than the lower so that when the mouth is closed it covers the top area of the lower lip (Figure 78). The opposite applies for a woman.

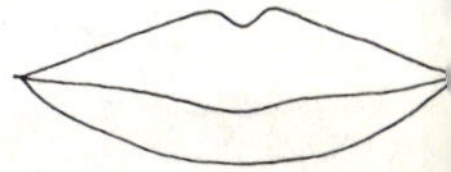

Figure 78

A woman whose lower lip is stronger than her upper likes a man to support and take care of her (Figure 79). She is likely to have a gentle nature and be good at housekeeping. A husband with a larger upper lip has a strong character, is capable of making decisions, and in family affairs will usually have the final say. If your upper lip is thin and your lower lip

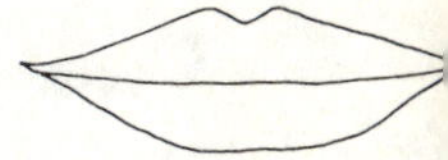

Figure 79

thick, you have a cunning nature, but if the upper lip is thick and the lower is thin, you will be poor. If both lips are thin, you deliberately make others unhappy, and although you may not speak rudely to someone's face you will make sure that he overhears your ill-natured words. Thick, well-balanced upper and lower lips denote a steady, honest nature which is reflected in speech. Someone with these lips can be trusted, unlike a cunning person who agrees to help then fails at the moment when he is most needed.

The luckiest lips are medium red in colour and glossy in appearance. They are a sign of a happy person who eats and dresses well. Lips the colour of chicken's liver denote a poor old age; lips which are very dark or almost black are a sign of disaster or serious illness in life.

SQUARE MOUTH (*Figure 80*)

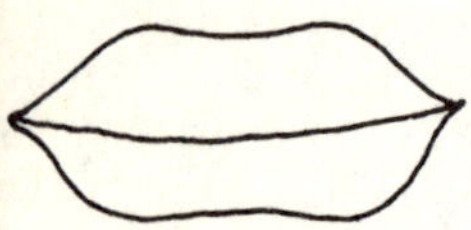

Figure 80

Both lips are thick, red in colour and the mouth is square. The teeth are bright and white. When smiling or laughing the lips are not drawn back to reveal the gums.

You will be respected, wealthy and lucky both with family and business. You are honest when dealing with friends and on good terms with your children and grandchildren. You will probably work as a merchant or a government officer.

4-CHARACTER MOUTH (*Figure 81*)

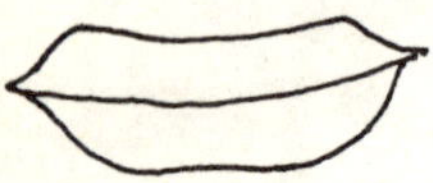

Figure 81

The sea corners can be clearly seen and are slightly turned upwards. Both lips are thick, well balanced, red in colour and moist to the touch. The teeth are also straight and the shape of the mouth is like the Chinese character for 4 (四).

You are clever, creative and artistically talented. You will be respected and wealthy during life and will have a happy old age. You are neither cunning nor dishonest and will have very happy relationships with your children and grandchildren.

NEW-MOON MOUTH (*Figure 82*)

Figure 82

The sea corners rise upwards and the mouth is shaped like a new moon. The lips are red, the teeth are white, and although the lips may be thin they still look beautiful.

You are suited to creative work and adept at debating, being able to maintain a strong line of argument. You will be rich and respected and will probably have a good wife and well-behaved children.

BLOWING-FIRE MOUTH (*Figure 83*)

Figure 83

The mouth always looks as if it is about to blow out a flame or fire since the corners of the lips slope downwards and there are no *ling*. The upper lip has a sharp point in the middle. Both lips are thin, the mouth is scrunched up, and the teeth protrude slightly and are irregularly shaped. The Chinese say that someone with this type of mouth can eat water melons since the teeth can scrape out the water melon seeds.

This mouth is a sign of a lonely person who will probably have a short life. If he does live long, his old age will be unhappy and he will generally suffer from resentment, particularly in regard to others. He delights in seeing those around him fail and gets a great deal of enjoyment from gossiping over the misfortunes of others.

SCRUNCHED MOUTH (*Figure 84*)

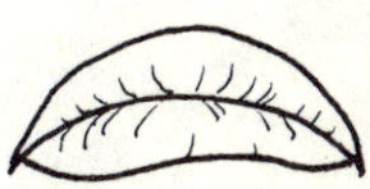

Figure 84

The sea corners slope downwards and the lips are thin and slightly wavy with a generally uneven appearance. They are dull in colour and dry to the touch.

These lips denote a lonely, difficult life; the owner will lose his wealth or business. He will have few friends, particularly in old age, and is capable of causing accidents or disasters.

FISH MOUTH (*Figure 85*)

Figure 85

The mouth is wide, the lips are thin and the sea corners slope down to a sharp point. The face with the fish mouth is usually pale.

You will be unsuccessful in business and cannot maintain your career even though you may have good economic backing from a family inheritance. You tend to be a target for gossip and are much talked about by other people. You will have to cope with many difficulties in old age.

LOTUS-LEAF MOUTH (*Figure 86*)

The mouth is long and thin, the colour dull, and the sea corners slope down slightly.

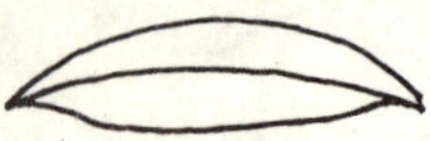

Figure 86

You have what the Chinese call a 'bad heart'. You like gossip and tend to conceal your own faults in order to avoid criticism. Although you are busy you will be unsuccessful in your career.

UNBALANCED MOUTH (Lopsided Mouth) (*Figure 87*)

One side of the mouth slopes down and the other up so the mouth is lopsided.

Figure 87

You like to talk about others, have a capacity for telling lies and enlarge or elaborate on what you have done. The Chinese say 'you like to speak through a magnifying glass'. Through your exaggeration you sometimes cheat yourself and others, however you feel very embarrassed when others reveal the truth. From time to time you may have a great deal of money, but you will not keep it for long. You are easily harmed or hurt by relationships with women.

CHERRY MOUTH (*Figure 88*)

The face is an average size and the mouth corners slope upwards. The lips are red and bright and the teeth small. The Chinese say that such teeth 'look like pomegranate seeds' since they grow close together and have a clear, crystal appearance. It is also said that a smile from a cherry mouth is 'like an open flower'.

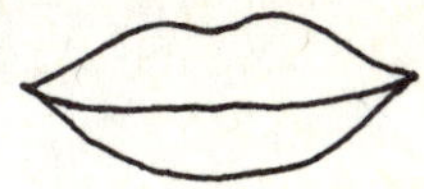

Figure 88

You are clever, wise and have a soft, gentle nature. You will always be wealthy and will know a respected person who helps you out in difficulties. The cherry mouth is an extremely fortunate feature in Chinese physiognomy, particularly for a woman.

The Teeth

Although the teeth do not a have an important function in physiognomy they can affect the shape of the mouth and therefore detract from the good qualities.

The teeth should be large, straight, long and grow close together (Figure 89). Small teeth are suitable so long as they are combined with a small mouth and a small face.

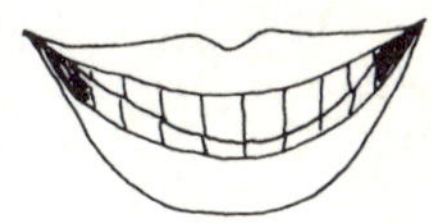

Figure 89

If the teeth are clean, white and strong then they are considered to be of the highest quality. The Chinese say that the colour of the teeth ought to be like 'white jade' which means that they have a transparent quality like that of pomegranate seeds. Someone with clear, well formed, crystal-white teeth is usually well dressed, has a good constitution and an honest disposition. He will be lucky during life and happy in old age. There ought to be between twenty-eight and thirty-two teeth; however, more than thirty-two is acceptable: it is better to have many teeth than few teeth. An accurate reading cannot be made solely from teeth but it is correct to say that a person with many teeth desires a job with high status. He will not be content with a low social or economic position.

Teeth that are strong but short in length are usually considered a bad sign in Chinese physiognomy. People with such teeth tend to be poor, hot-tempered and will easily ruin what they are doing through impatience and a tendency to abandon a problem which has been half solved. A smile or a laugh which reveals both upper and lower teeth is a sign that the owner will suffer at the hands of others. A woman with such teeth may be a prostitute, but if her mouth is well formed and her features well balanced she will have a more auspicious fortune than a prostitute.

If your teeth have many gaps you will be unsuccessful in business, and even though your teeth may be straight and strong the money which you earn will be easily lost or spent (Figure 90). Irregular teeth signify unsuccessful business, loss of money, a short life, or possibly death by accident. Someone whose front teeth are at angles to each other cannot keep a secret and will struggle to find a good job and save money. If one of your front teeth sticks outwards and the other inwards, you are continually on the move, lacking a permanent home base.

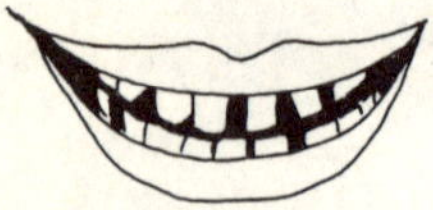

Figure 90

If the rest of the teeth are uneven (rabbit teeth) this denotes a poor life; such a person will cause disasters or trouble. If all the teeth grow in different directions, are uneven and sharp or pointed, the owner is lacking in virtue and will cause many accidents both minor and serious (Figure 91). A combination of uneven teeth and well-balanced features signifies an outspoken person who discusses others' faults and behaviour; he has a critical nature. The Chinese refer to ugly teeth as 'ghost teeth'; they say that they belong to someone who is poor and accident-prone and who will have a short life. A brace can correct these teeth and to some extent may improve the physiognomy. Such teeth are usually seen in a badly proportioned face.

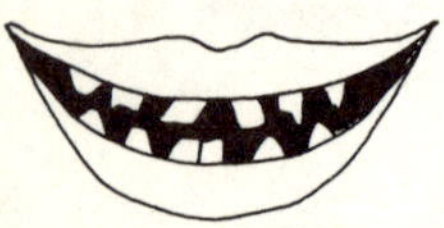

Figure 91

The Tongue

A good tongue is large and wide, and in speaking does not loll in the mouth but moves in a lively way. A short, sleepy tongue is unlucky. Someone who can lick the tip of his nose will be wealthy and respected. A tongue which is long and narrow when stuck out is considered an unlucky sign. If a long, narrow tongue is combined with the inability to lick the tip of the nose it is a sign of a cunning nature. A short, rough tongue belongs to a person who suffers from bad luck. A sharp, short tongue denotes a greedy, avaricious nature. A man with a sharp, long tongue is considered to be excellent in argument but is always plotting how to cheat others.

The tongue should be deep red, since this signifies high status and respectability. If the tongue is smoky blue or black, white or grey the owner will receive little respect. A black tongue is an indication of a dishonest person. A tongue with wrinkles down its length is a sign of honesty, but wrinkles running across the tongue are a sign of someone who is ill-mannered and outspoken; even when requested he will not temper his words. Crossing lines on the tongue denote success in business.

Lines from the Nose – Fa Ling

There are various lines which run from the nose down to the mouth and these are known as *fa ling*. Each one will give a different reading. If the lines from the nose cannot be seen clearly it is a sign of a troublesome life with little job satisfaction (Figure 92). If unclear *fa ling* are combined with dull, sleepy eyes, a short life will be predicted.

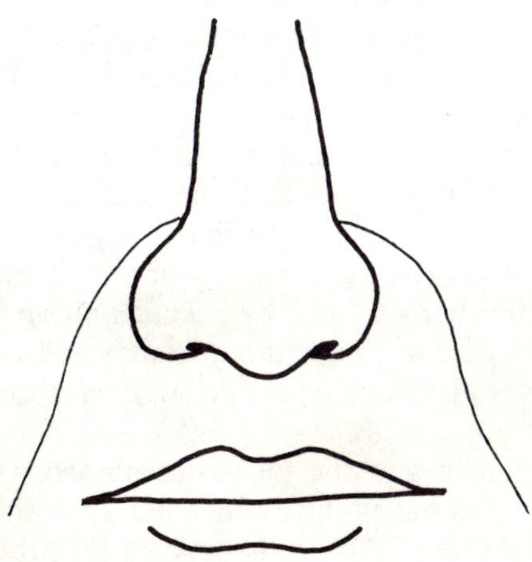

Figure 92

Someone with a mole on the *fa ling* is likely to lose any inheritance from his family and to keep his distance from relatives since they always end up arguing when they meet (Figure 93). He is not happy in his job and aspires to a better position; his discontent results in career problems. He will experience at least one great loss or serious accident in his life.

If your *fa ling* run parallel to each other or if there is a subsidiary line branching out from the first line, your father or mother is not your natural parent (Figure 94). You will also find it difficult to hold on to an inheritance from your parents. *Fa ling* which run from the sides of the nose to the corners of the mouth are in what the Chinese call a 'locking position'; someone with these lines will die of hunger or suffer a serious disaster around fifty years of age (Figure 95). There is a story in Chinese history which dates from the beginning of the Christian period of a man named Liong See Yee, thought to be a god of wealth by the citizens of his town. Although he had a locking line he was fortunate since he had a red mole on the tip of his tongue. If the locking lines are combined with a mole on the tip of the tongue the Chinese say that it represents two dragons scratching a pearl; the *fa ling* are the dragons, and the mole is the pearl. The very fact that Liong See Yee had such a mole saved him from the unfortunate disaster which would have otherwise occurred. As a result he was wealthy throughout life and did not die of hunger (Figure 96).

Fa ling running to the mouth from the nose then continuing on to the chin are called *t'eng* snake (Figure 97). A person with this line pattern will die early if he is rich, but if he is poor he will eventually die from hunger or by accidental poisoning. Frequently he will be without friends and will probably lose his money or belongings through an accident.

Locking lines at the mouth combined with lines running from below the eye to the area of the mouth are an indication of death by poisoning, either gas or food poisoning (Figure 98). This is likely to happen around the age of fifty.

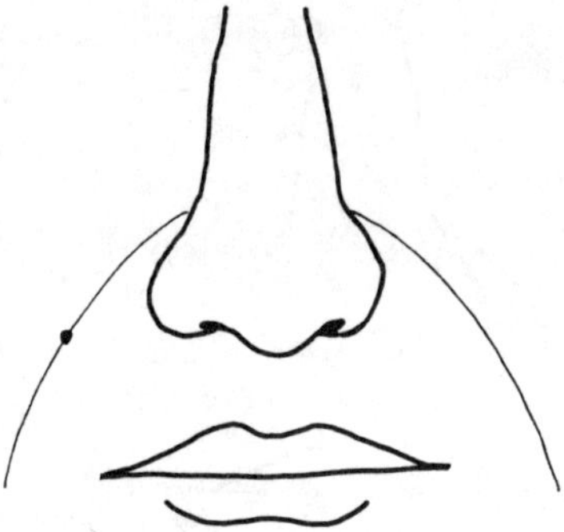

Figure 93

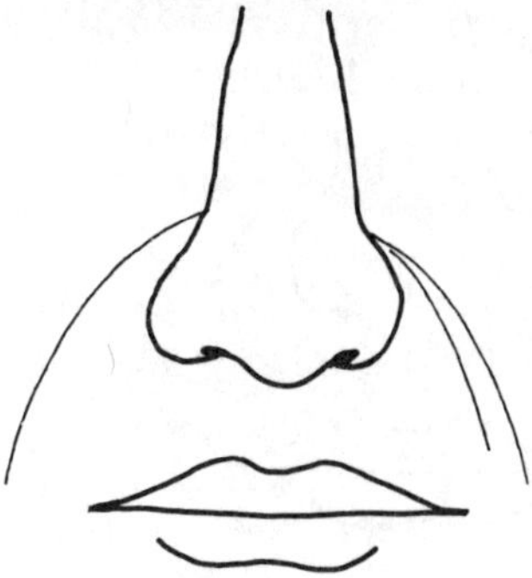

Figure 94

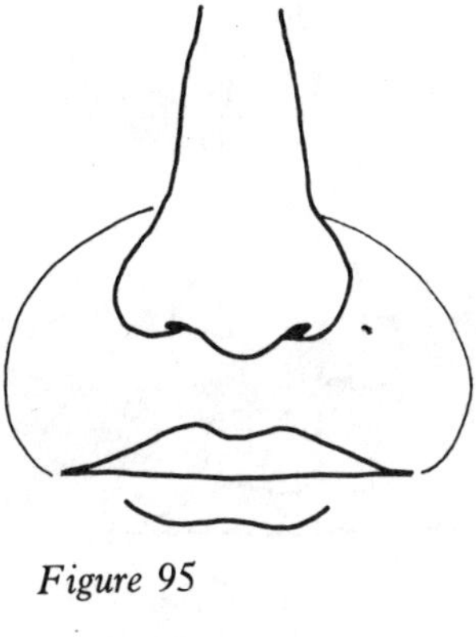

Figure 95

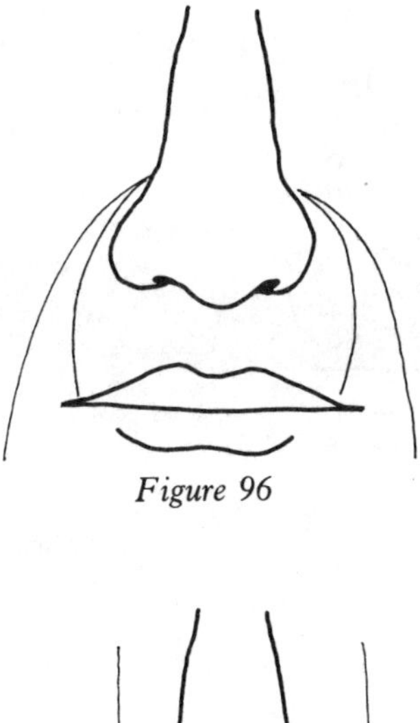

Figure 96

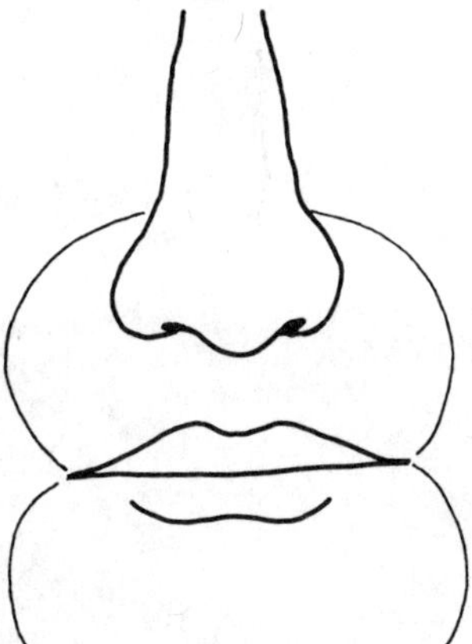

Figure 97

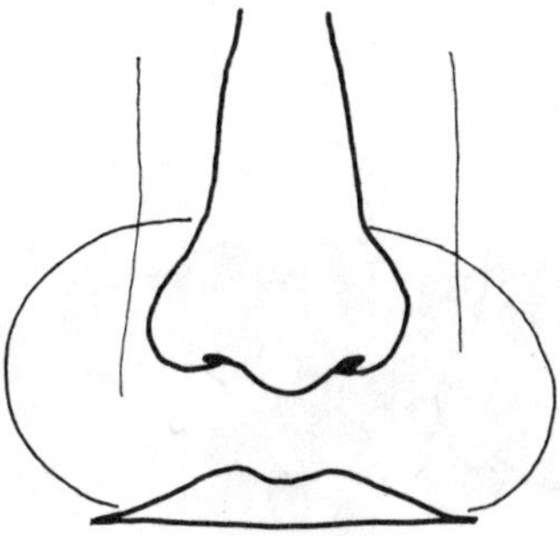

Figure 98

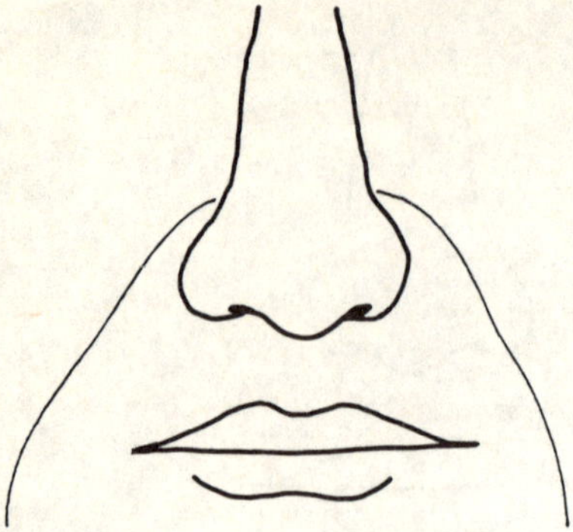

Figure 99

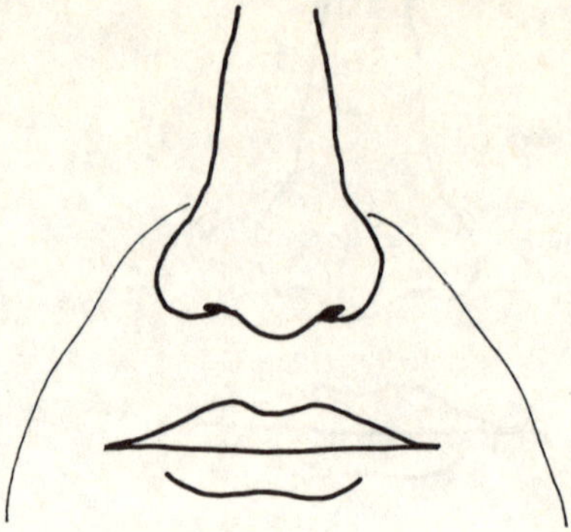

Figure 100

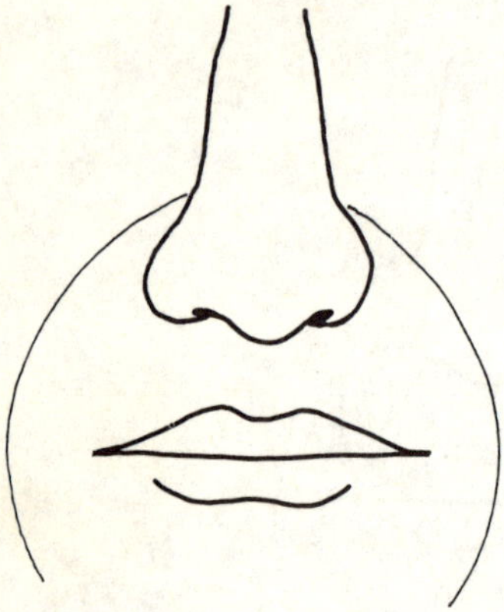

Figure 101

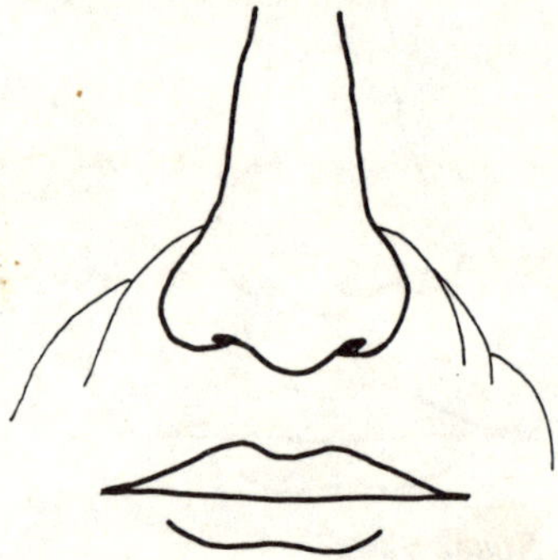

Figure 102

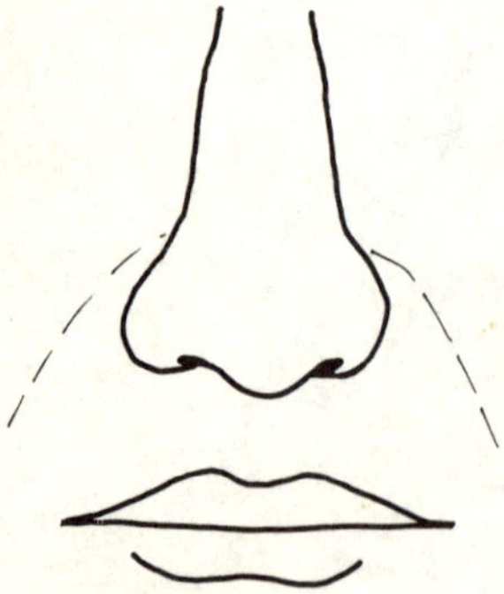

Figure 103

If the *fa ling* become wider, sloping at an angle to the nose, you may not be rich but you will certainly be famous (Figure 99); perhaps you will become a director of a committee, a commissioner of police or a successful artist. If you are well known and wealthy, your money is likely to come from commerce. If these lines extend to well below the mouth, you may be wealthy and respected but will have a lonely old age (Figure 100). *Fa ling* which curve inwards to a locking position below one sea corner are a sign of a long life (Figure 101).

Branching *fa ling* are an indication that you are entering an unlucky period; even though you may be well educated you will not be able to find a good job (Figure 102). You may have to leave home or go abroad to find a suitable well-paid job; nevertheless, your situation will not be much improved. When the *fa ling* are broken, missing or faint, you may go through lucky periods but they will not last long. Throughout your life you will never be satisfied with your career (Figure 103). Dull eyes combined with broken or indistinct *fa ling* signify a short life.

The Emperor and the Copper Mine

During the Han dynasty there lived an important civil official known as Ten T'ung. The Emperor Wen Ti was seriously concerned about the *fa ling* on Ten T'ung's face, and so he summoned the court's fortune-teller, Hsu Fu. Hsu Fu examined Ten T'ung's *fa ling* and proclaimed them to be in a locking position; the only accurate prediction he could give was that Ten T'ung would die of hunger.

The Emperor was distressed to hear this news and searched his mind to think of a way to prevent this terrible forecast. He came upon the brilliant idea of giving Ten T'ung a mountain which was a rich source of copper. Ten T'ung could mine the copper to make coins with which he could buy lots of food. The Emperor was now content since he had saved Ten T'ung from this terrible fate, and Ten T'ung quickly became a rich man.

After Wen Ti's death, a new Emperor, Chang Ti, succeeded to the throne. Unfortunately he was unaware of his predecessor's reasons for giving the copper mine to Ten T'ung, and, satisfied that this civil official was sufficiently wealthy, he reclaimed the mine. Ten T'ung immediately lost the source of his wealth and was left to live off the money he had accumulated. When this supply dried up Ten T'ung was left destitute. Soon he died of starvation.

8
The Five Features: The Ears

The ears are not normally thought of as an important feature; however, they are the only feature which remains immobile and therefore can never lie. Thus, they are important in Chinese physiognomy.

The ear should be pink, white or slightly red, and bright and clean in appearance. The skin of the ear should not be shaded or blotchy. A large ear is more auspicious than a small one, the only exception being the chess ear (see Figure 110). The outline of the ear is called the wheel and is divided into three parts. The top part is called the heaven wheel, the middle part the human wheel and the bottom part the earth wheel. The inner ridge of the ear is referred to as the ear line, the bottom, fleshy part of the ear is known as the ear pearl, and the centre of the ear is referred to as the earhole (Figure 104).

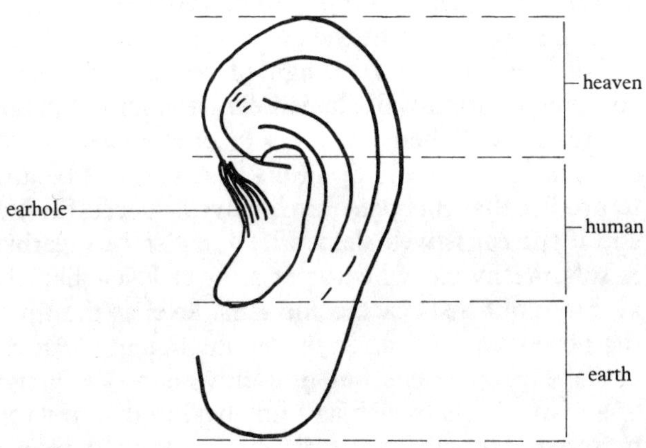

Figure 104

The ideal ear should grow close to the head and be set on a level between the eyebrow and the tip of the nose. The wheel and ear line should be smooth and unbroken and the ear should feel slightly fleshy. The ancient fortune-tellers called this type of ear the 'five-fortune ear'. The five fortunes are luck, long life, good fortune, a comfortable house and a happy family. Someone with the five-fortune ear has a lucky nature and will be a good friend. A good reading will not be given for an ear which has an indistinct ear line or wheel, patchy skin colouring and is smaller or larger than the standard size. Someone with this ear is likely to have few friends and a bossy nature. An ear which does not have an ear pearl and is positioned below the level of the eyebrow is a sign of an unpleasant nature; the owner is possibly caught up in theft or drugs.

Someone with a small and permanently grey or dirty ear will be involved in illegal dealings. He cannot be trusted to keep a secret and may possibly commit treason. If the top of the ear is at a higher level than the eyebrow and the ear pearl at a higher level than the tip of the nose, the owner is intelligent but his friends find him difficult to deal with since he is an exhibitionist. Although he is capable, his disposition does not appeal to prospective employers, and therefore he has difficulty finding a suitable job. In addition, he frequently quarrels with his family and is consequently subject to considerable worry.

If the lower part of the ear is on a level with the tip of the nose, it is a sign of success; if this is combined with a well-shaped ear, it is an indication of creativity. When you see someone whose bottom ear is in line with the tip of his nose you will be able to predict that this person will have a successful life, and if the ear is well shaped he will also be creative. A soft, fleshy ear which is at a lower level than the eyebrow but just reaches the same level as the tip of the nose is an indication of low intelligence. An ear of these proportions but unevenly shaped is a sign of a man who is foolish and involved in disreputable pastimes. He will find it difficult to alter or reform his life.

A pointed heaven wheel belongs to someone who seems to be quite cruel, and if his inner line curves out towards the ear wheel he also has a destructive nature. A rounded heaven wheel and an inner line which grows outwards and upwards towards the heaven wheel signifies a difficult life and few children. If the ear is whiter or paler than the rest of the face the owner will be famous. An ear which is red or pink and has glossy appearance belongs to someone who is clever and reasonably wealthy, whereas a dark red or grey ear is considered unfortunate. Any dirty tinges on the ear which cannot be washed away are a sign of a person who is poor and little respected. If you develop dirty patches on your ears, take care since this means that you are about to enter a period of bad luck.

A thick, hard ear is a sign of good luck, but an ear that is paper thin signifies a brief and impoverished life. Ears of a different size denote troubled actions and disturbed plans. If the heaven line on the left ear grows away from your head, you have a bad relationship with your father; if the heaven line on the right ear grows away from your head, you have a bad relationship with your mother. The opposite will apply for women. Any unusual curves on the ear will detract from a good reading even if the colour of the ear is perfect.

We have included thirteen common ear shapes from which it is possible to make a reading.

GOLD EAR (*Figure 105*)

This ear is set slightly higher than the eyebrow and the heaven wheel and inner line are close together. The ear is square-shaped and the pearl feels hard. You will also notice that the lines of the outer wheel and the inner ring are distinct and the ear is usually paler than the face.

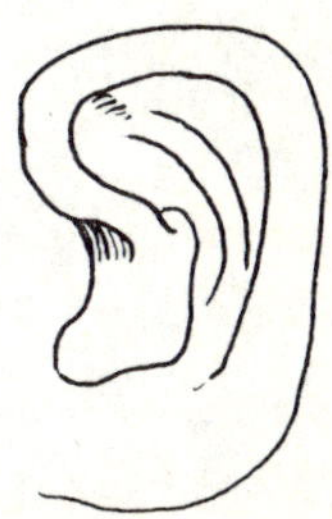

Figure 105

You are clever and creative, and will always be successful whether you have an intellectual job or a job in the arts. If you have a gold shape you will also be wealthy, although you will have a quarrelsome relationship with your wife and children. It is considered unlucky if a wood-shaped person has this type of ear as he will be lonely and poor in old age.

WOOD EAR (*Figure 106*)

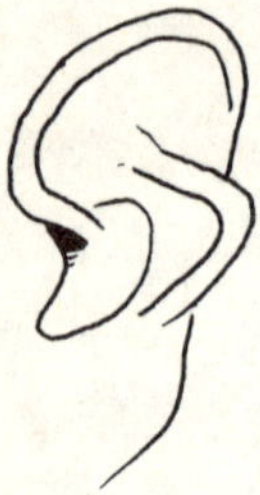

Figure 106

The heaven wheel slopes upwards and the inner ring grows out beyond the outer wheel. The whole ear feels thin, is dull in colour and has no ear pearl. The upper part of the ear in the area of the heaven wheel is larger than the earth wheel, and in general the shape of the wheel does not conform to the standard.

You are little respected and will have a difficult life; your reading will be improved if all your other features are well formed. The wood ear is particularly suited to the wood-shaped person and signifies a fairly comfortable old age. An inauspicious reading would be given for someone with a wood ear and a gold or earth shape.

WATER EAR (*Figure 107*)

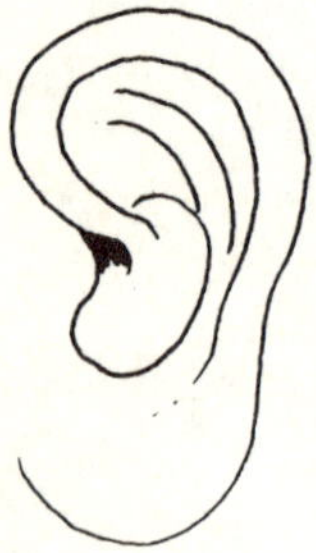

Figure 107

Water ears are thick, round in shape and set close to the head. They have an ear pearl and are usually whiter than the face and higher in position than the eyebrow.

They are a sign of intelligence and quick wits. You are not easily flustered and can be patient when circumstances are not running smoothly. The water ear does not combine well with the fire-shaped person.

FIRE EAR (*Figure 108*)

The heaven wheel curves to a point and is slightly higher than the eyebrow. The inner line grows outward over the wheel and the ear is long and hard. This ear is suitable for a fire-shaped person.

You are probably respected but lonely, since you find it difficult to accept advice whether it is given by an enemy or a friend. You will usually have a troubled relationship with your wife and family and tend to be at the beck and call of others. Since you believe you are always right you are frequently involved in arguments. A fire ear in combination with the gold- or water-shaped person means a poor and short life.

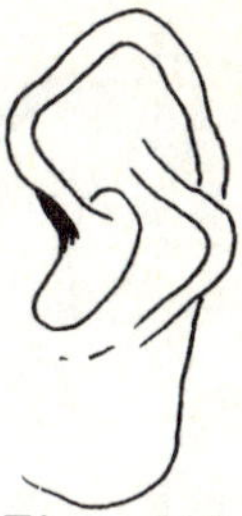

Figure 108

EARTH EAR (*Figure 109*)

This ear is fat and large; the ear pearl is large and the outer wheel and inner ring are well formed and unbroken. This ear is usually red or pink in colour and has a glossy sheen.

The earth ear signifies a long and prosperous life with good, stable family relationships. A combination of earth ear and wood shape denotes a difficult, lonely life if the owner is wealthy.

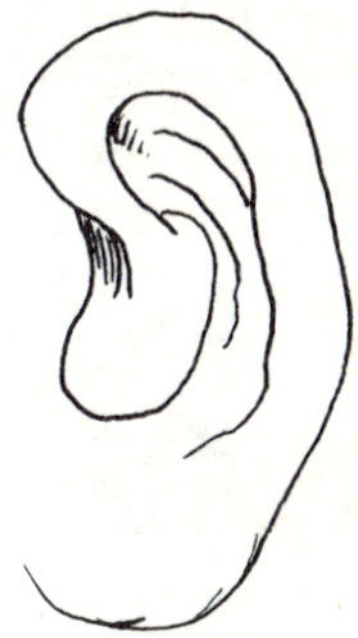

Figure 109

CHESS EAR (*Figure 110*)

This ear is small, round, thick and hard. The ear is whiter than the face and is set slightly higher than the eyebrow.

You have an enterprising nature and will be particularly successful in middle age. The chess ear does not combine well with a wood-shaped person; someone with these characteristics will be unsuccessful in his actions. However, the chess ear is well matched with a gold shape since it signifies good fortune in marriage.

Figure 110

LONG EAR (Touching Shoulder Ear) (*Figure 111*)

The ear pearl is long and the ear is thick and fat. The ear is at a higher level than the eyebrow and the skin is clear and glossy.

It is very rare to see such an ear since the Chinese say it usually belongs to a rich and powerful man; it is the type of ear one might see on an emperor or king.

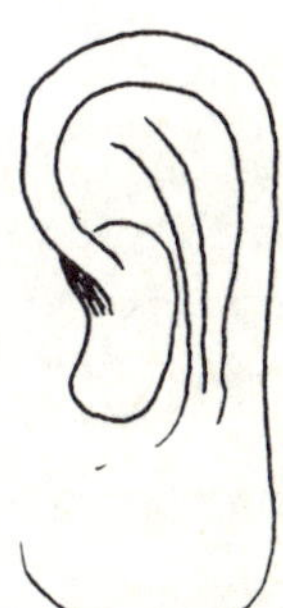

Figure 111

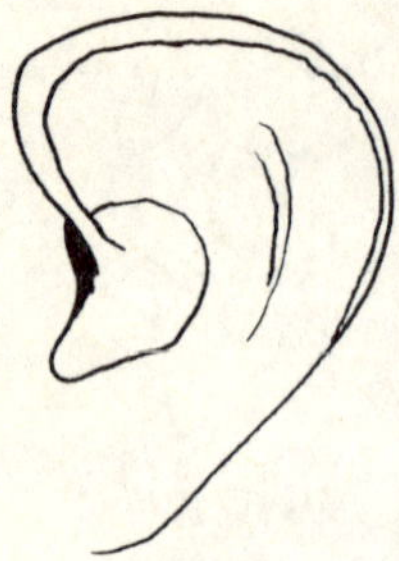

Figure 112

CATCHING-WIND EAR (*Figure 112*)

The catching-wind ear is so called because it grows away from the head.

This ear usually belongs to someone who leaves his country at an early age or has to live apart from his family. He will be satisfied in youth but unless he marries his middle and old age will be poor and lonely. An ear which has all the characteristics of the catching-wind ear except that it is thinner and has an indistinct ear line is known as an 'open-flower ear'. This type of ear denotes an unlucky and poverty-stricken life.

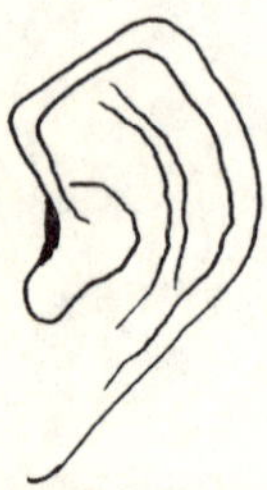

Figure 113

UPPER FORWARD EAR (*Figure 113*)

This ear is S-shaped, but while the heaven wheel slopes forward the pearl bends backwards. The lines of the inner ring and outer wheel are indistinct.

Someone with this ear will have a lonely, difficult life; although he may pass through wealthy periods, disaster and accidents will frequently come his way.

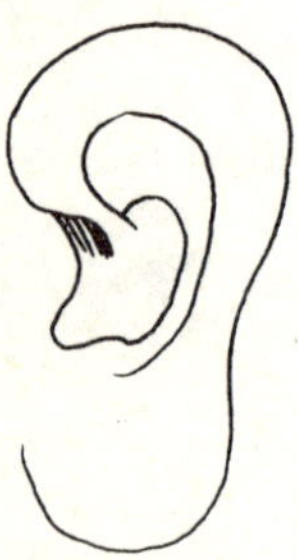

Figure 114

PIG EAR (*Figure 114*)

The pig ear has no wheel, no inner ring and no definite shape. It feels thick and soft. It may grow forward or backwards; its only definite characteristic is soft muscle.

This ear is associated with dull eyes and a hot temper. The owner is likely to die by accident or be caught up in a disaster. Although many opportunities come his way they tend to disappear before he has a chance to take advantage of them. Even if he wins money he will lose it quickly.

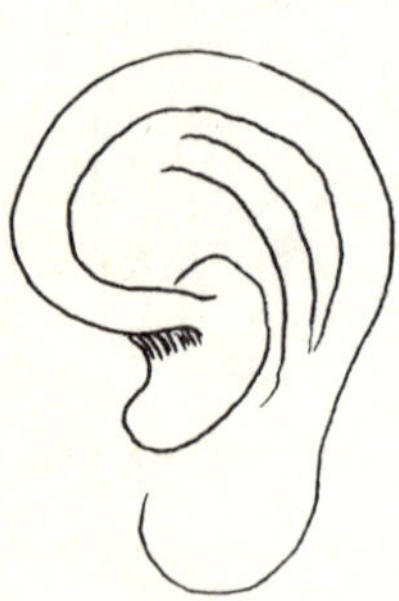

Figure 115

RAT EAR (*Figure 115*)

This ear is small and does not grow in a standard direction. It has no ear pearl and the outer wheel is tightly curled. It is usually on the same level as the eyebrow but occasionally it is higher.

The rat ear is a sign of an evil, cunning and avaricious nature. Someone with a combination of rat ear and ill-balanced features is likely to fall foul of the law; it is commonplace for him to be in some sort of trouble. His bad fortune will be mitigated if the other four features are well balanced, although he will have a short life.

TIGER EAR (*Figure 116*)

The ear is thick, hard, small and tightly curled. The lines of the outer wheel and inner ring cannot be distinguished easily and are sometimes broken. Tiger ears cannot be seen when looking directly at the face.

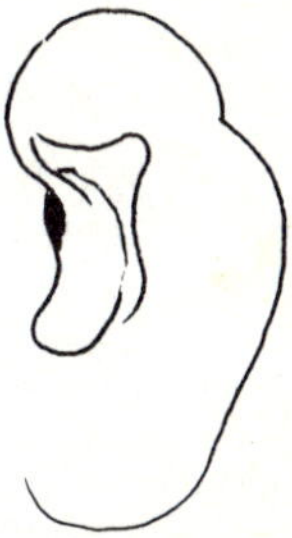

Figure 116

You are honest and straightforward and people usually hold you in awe because of your powerful character. This type of ear is suitable for a thin or short person but signifies a short life if it is found on a fat person.

PORCUPINE (ARROW PIG) EAR (*Figure 117*)

The top of the wheel is at a higher level than the eyebrow and the upper part is wider than the lower. This ear is hard and straight with a strong appearance.

Figure 117

You are clever and wise and will probably be famous. You are a wanderer and have difficulty putting down any roots; you are also likely to lose any money you may have inherited.

9 The Face

Ancient Chinese fortune-tellers have distinguished 130 positions on the face, and from these physiognomists, over the centuries, have picked out the fifty most important. These positions include the Twelve Palaces, which cover different areas of the whole face (see pp. 110–15), the Thirteen Positions, which run in a line from the forehead to the chin, and the Twelve Earthly Stems, which form a circle around the face (see pp. 118–19). The Thirteen Positions and the Twelve Palaces enable the fortune-teller to make predictions up to the age of seventy, and the Twelve Earthly Stems provide readings from the ages of seventy to a hundred.

The Thirteen Positions of the Face

The centre line of the face is divided into thirteen positions (Figure 118) as follows:

1	*t'ien chung*	6	*shan ken*	10	*jen chung*
2	*t'ien t'ing*	7	*nien shang*	11	*shui hsing*
3	*ssu k'ung*	8	*shou shang*	12	*ch'eng chiang*
4	*chung cheng*	9	*chun t'ou*	13	*ti ko*
5	*yin t'ang*				

1 T'IEN CHUNG

This is the area that covers the top half of the forehead. A good reading can be given if the *t'ien chung* is smooth and rounded and the skin clear and bright. The surface of the skin should be free from cuts and scars. Someone with a good *t'ien chung* had a very happy youth, his parents will live to an old age and their relationship will always be amicable. Grey or black marks on the forehead and an uneven hairline

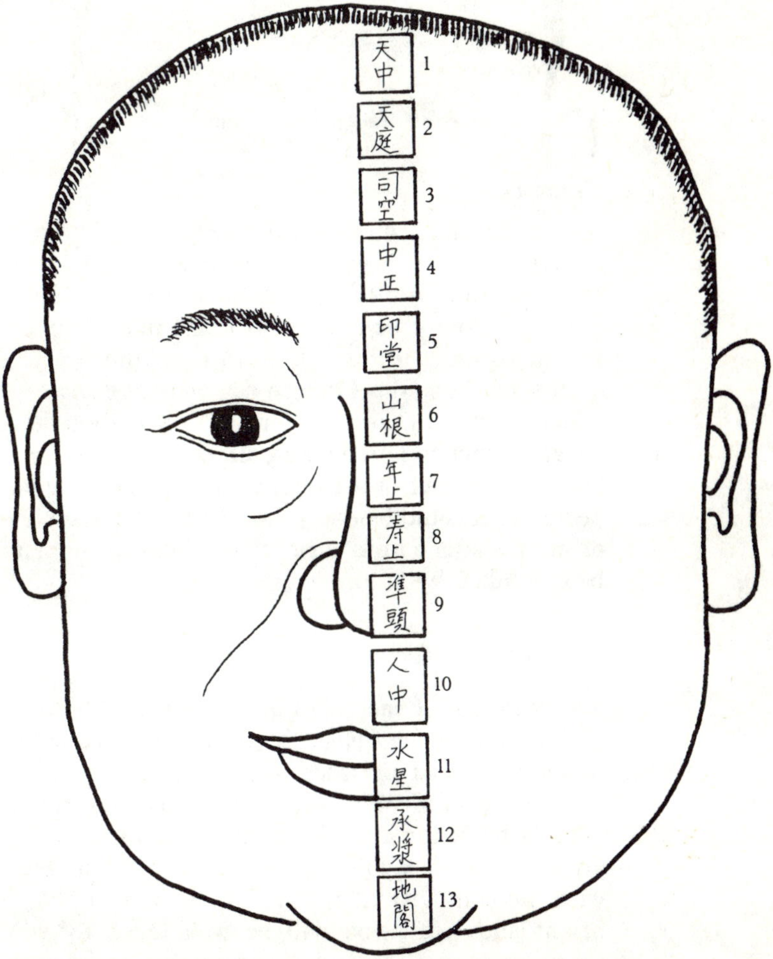

Figure 118 The Thirteen Positions

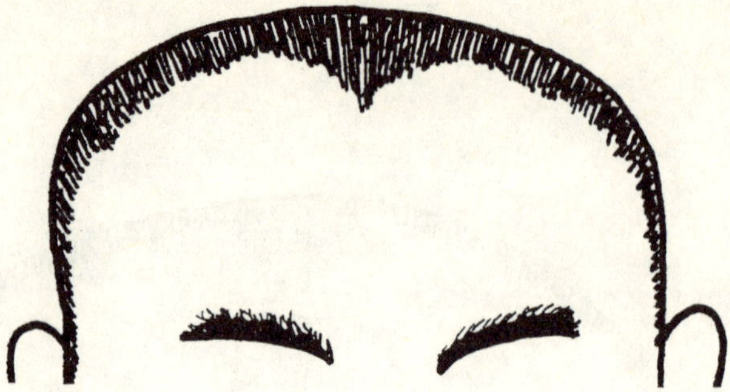

Figure 119

denote bad luck during youth (Figure 119) due to poverty or family arguments. Hair which grows to a point on the *t'ien chung* indicates that your father will die before your mother. If a line like a vein can be felt running through the centre of the forehead to the hairline, the Chinese say it is the *shan ken* which is running into the forest. This is thought to be an unlucky sign. During life you will suffer at least one disaster or accident which will arrive unexpectedly. It could be that just as you are on the verge of success after a long-term project you will suddenly be overtaken by failure.

2 T'IEN T'ING

The meaning of the *t'ien t'ing* is basically the same as that of the *t'ien chung*; the only difference is that this area is read in order to predict your mother's fortune, whereas the *t'ien chung* is read to predict your father's fortune. An accurate reading will be given if the *t'ien t'ing* is examined in conjunction with the complexion. If the area of the *t'ien t'ing* is bright and clear, you will be well loved by your parents and will always have an important friend to help you in difficulties. Grey colouring in the *t'ien t'ing* is referred to by Chinese fortune-tellers as a 'black cloud', and is a sign that nobody will believe you when you tell the truth. A green tinge is an indication of an unfortunate event within the coming two weeks; therefore take care until this green colour disappears.

3 SSU K'UNG

Again the meaning is almost the same as that of the *t'ien t'ing*, but this area will be dealt with in greater detail in relation to the Twelve Palaces (see p. 111). A glossy complexion which is yellow or red in colour is a sign of a well respected and fortunate person. Grey marks on the skin are an indication that you are entering a period of bad luck. Such a mark can appear at any time in life, so care must be taken until it disappears. During this unlucky period you may put considerable effort into your work but will not succeed.

4 CHUNG CHENG

A *chung cheng* which is smooth, rounded, bright and clear is a sign of an early career and success in business, whereas a dented *chung cheng* is an indication of low intellect. Someone with a black mole, cuts or scars from previous accidents, or large lumps or spots in this area has no patience, and although he may make many plans he will always be prevented access to necessary people and places. He will not get on with his friends but will never understand why.

5 YIN T'ANG

The *yin t'ang* should not be dented, lumpy or too rounded. A *yin t'ang* which has a healthy glow is an indication of a large family inheritance. Your business will run smoothly and success will come easily. A narrow gap between the eyebrows signifies loss of goods and business failure (Figure 120), and eyebrows which meet in the middle are a sign of an unlucky and difficult life. Physiognomists say that someone with the latter type of eyebrow lacks noble characteristics. He is likely to be caught up in crime; even if he escapes prosecution he is held in very low esteem by other people.

A birthmark or scar on the *yin t'ang* is a sign of adoption. A black mole in the centre of the *yin t'ang*

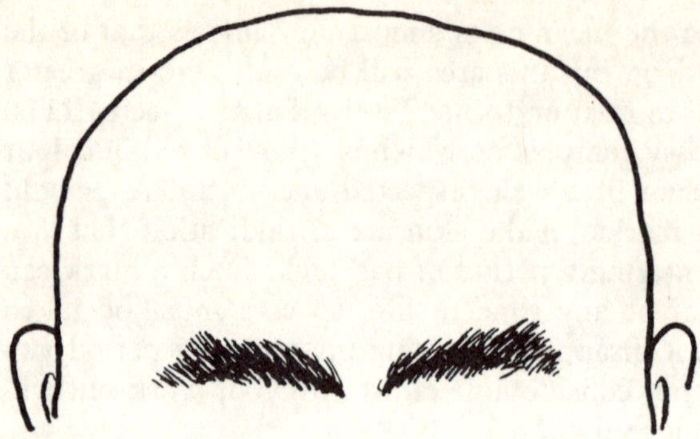

Figure 120

heralds a long-term illness, whereas a black mole to the side of this area is an indication that you will spend some time in jail at least once in your life. A prison sentence can be predicted if there are black moles on the forehead.

Two wrinkles in the *yin t'ang* sloping outwards towards each eye are a sign of a difficult life and failure to achieve fame or fortune (Figure 121). However, if these wrinkles appear after forty years of age and the other features are well balanced, your luck is likely to change. A woman with these wrinkles has a jealous nature and finds it difficult to settle down to a domestic life.

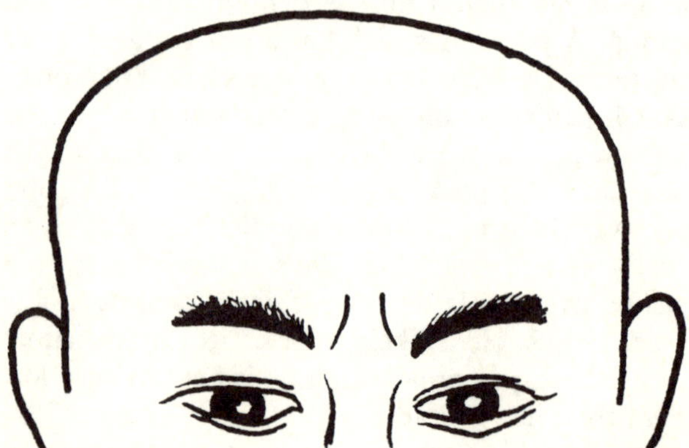

Figure 121

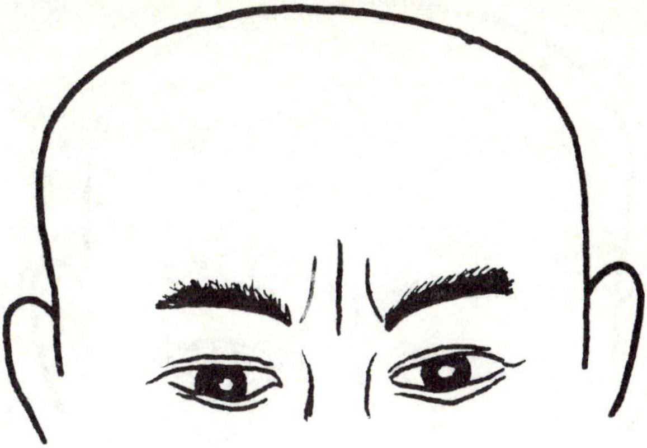

Figure 122

An additional line running straight down between these two lines is an indication of an anxious and tense character (Figure 122). Someone with three such lines will also have an unstable relationship with his wife; he ought to take care in middle age, since he is likely to have an accident. If the lines slope outwards at an angle you are not particularly quick witted (Figure 123). You will begin a career and marry late in life, but will have very few good opportunities and will probably be poor. You frequently grumble about your unlucky circumstances.

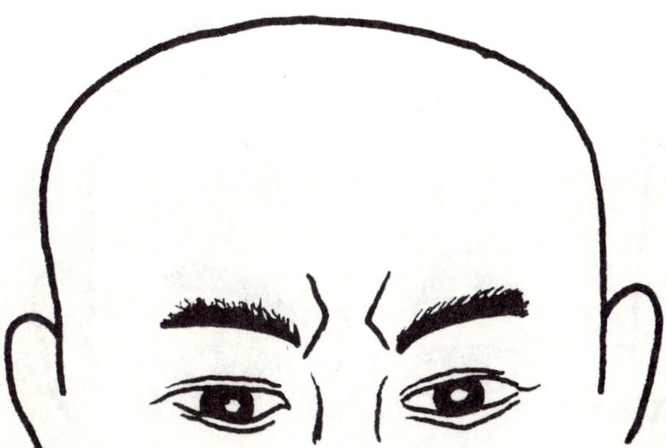

Figure 123

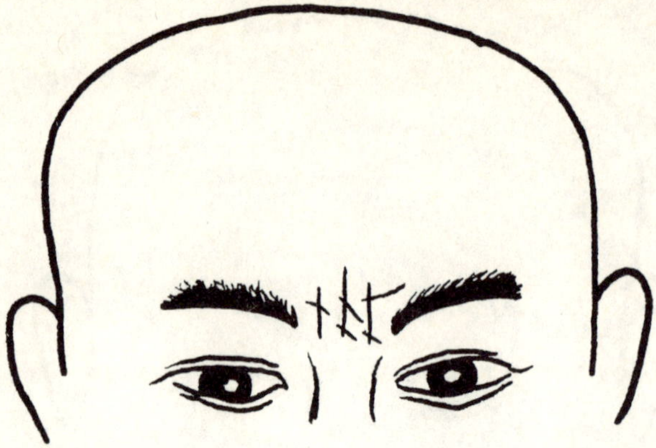

Figure 124

Many lines crossing in the *yin t'ang* area are an unlucky sign (Figure 124). You will struggle for success and your parents will succumb to a quick death. Deep wrinkles are an indication that you cannot control your temper and easily offend others. The majority of people with these particular lines will die at the age of thirty.

One line running through the middle of the *yin t'ang* is referred to as the hanging-needle line (Figure 125). It is thought to be an unlucky line, since it denotes poverty, anxiety and worry. If this line is particularly deep you will have a short life.

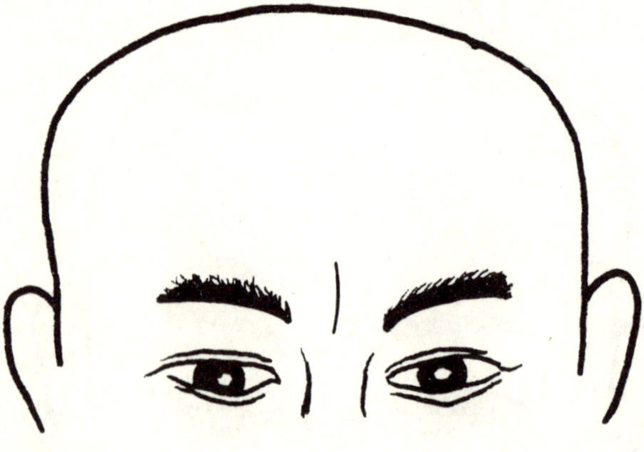

Figure 125

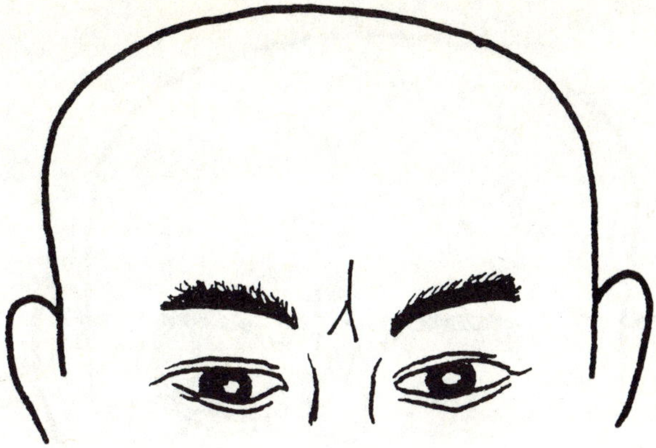

Figure 126

An additional line branching out from the hanging-needle line will increase your fortune (Figure 126). A respected and wealthy man will offer help if you run into trouble.

If one of the two lines in this area curves towards the eyebrow at its upper point, you have brought shame on your family (Figure 127). After this initial deed you will regain their respect through good behaviour, and by doing this your luck will improve. It is, however, necessary that you always take care in the future.

Loss of parents or family at an early age (Figure

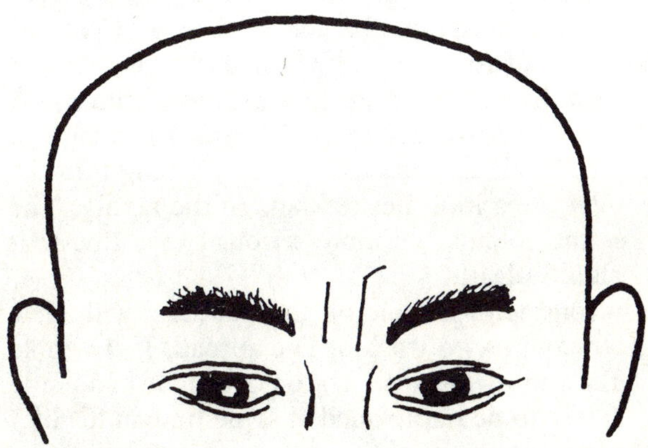

Figure 127

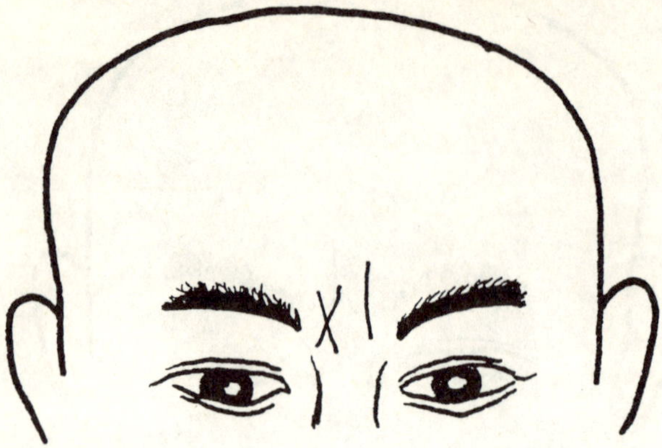

Figure 128

128) is recognized by two of the three lines crossing each other in the *yin t'ang* area. Around the age of forty you will realize that your hobbies are either criminal or a health hazard and therefore decide to abandon them.

6 SHAN KEN

This is the border between the heaven and the human areas (see pp. 115–18), and also the border between the yin side of the face (the right-hand side) and the yang side of the face (the left-hand side). This area should not be flat, since contact between the heaven and human areas must be maintained, and yin and yang must be able to meet and balance each other. If this area is grey or dark, take care of your health since you are in a period of illness. A green tinge to the side of the *shan ken* is a sign of adultery. A black tinge to the skin running into the *nien shang* area indicates sickness in the family. The darker the colour, the more serious the sickness; it may signify death.

Someone with a mole on the *shan ken* will leave his own country to work or live abroad. If the mole is at the top of the *shan ken* on the right-hand side he is likely to be imprisoned at some time in his life. A mole on one side of the *shan ken* is an indication of stomach trouble.

7 NIEN SHANG

Although this has been mentioned in relation to the nose, a mole on the *nien shang* also indicates troubled relationships. Your partner will either fall ill, cause emotional problems or bring you shame. A mole is also a sign of stomach trouble even if you are healthy and strongly built.

A man who has straight lines running down the length of the *nien shang* will not be the true father of his children. If this area is a dark smoky colour, one of his family will be ill.

8 SHOU SHANG

This area has already been mentioned in relation to the nose (see p. 70). In addition, a protruding bone on the *shou shang* is a sign of an unsuccessful business venture. Someone with a mole or a dirty mark on the *shou shang* or *nien shang* will have trouble with female relationships. If a woman has a mole on her *nien shang* or *shou shang*, her husband will be prone to illness. Someone with clear, bright skin on both sides of the *shou shang* and the *nien shang* dresses well and has a strong stomach for eating and drinking.

9 CHUN T'OU (Nose Tip)

It is unfortunate if the tip of the nose is thin or sharp, or if there are black smudgy marks on it, since these detract from the good fortune of the *chun t'ou*. Black or enlarged pores and hairs on the tip of the nose denote a difficult life.

10 JEN CHUNG

Readings are taken of the *jen chung* when considering the fortune of a person's children. If the upper area is narrow, the lower area wide and the lines not too deep or too flat, you will have many healthy children and be highly respected and wealthy (Figure 129). If the *jen chung* is wide at its upper point, narrow at its lower point and has a shallow appearance, you

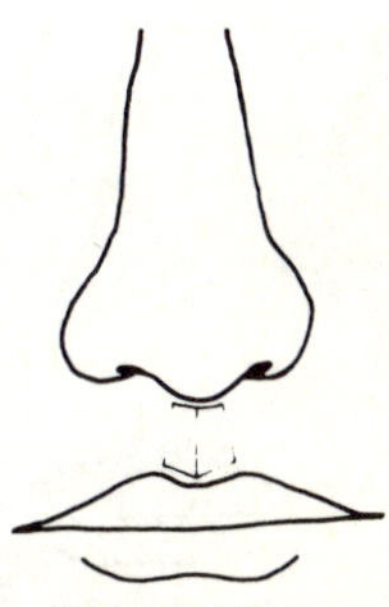

Figure 129

will have very few children; you also are selfish and bad-tempered (Figure 130). Your ill manners make it difficult for you to form friendships, and you have criminal tendencies. Although your life will be long, your family relationships will be unstable and you will be lonely in your old age. A slanting or bent *jen chung* is an indication of a childless and deceitful person (Figure 131).

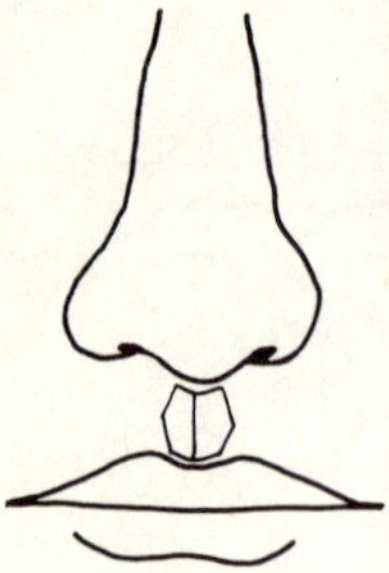

Figure 130

A straight line running through the *jen chung* denotes the advent of children late in life. A *jen chung* which bends or is narrow at its upper and lower points but wide in the middle indicates unlucky periods after middle age (Figure 132). If the *jen chung* has a line running across it or just inside it, you will have trouble with your children; you may have difficulty conceiving, in which case you are likely to adopt. Someone whose *jen chung* is uneven or irregular in appearance will have no children and will encounter poverty and loneliness.

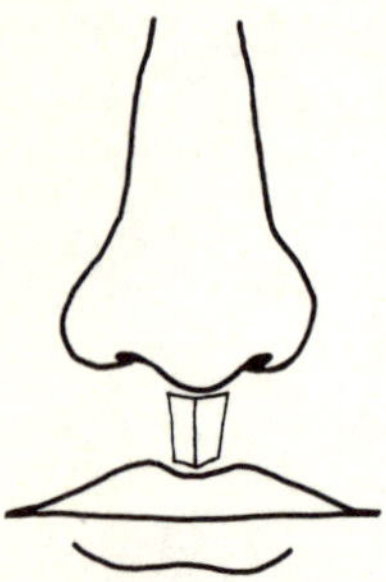

Figure 131

An examination of the *jen chung* indicates the sex of your offspring. A *jen chung* which is deep and narrow at its upper point and wide at its lower point, with distinct lines, denotes more sons than daughters. Indistinct lines and a deep *jen chung* denotes more daughters than sons. Some people have no *jen chung*; therefore they will have no children. The *jen chung* gradually becomes clearer as you become older, so an accurate reading from the *jen chung* cannot be made for a child.

11 SHUI HSING

The *shui hsing* is the area of the upper and lower lips. We can see from the lips whether a person is healthy, trustworthy, whether he or she is in a position of power, and whether, for a woman, she is a chatterbox. Someone with a hanging lip and a dry complexion is slow to react and is unlikely to live beyond sixty.

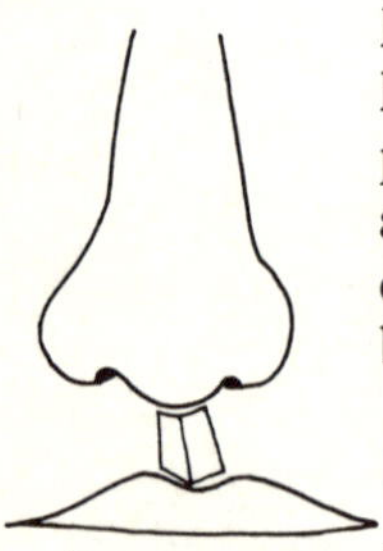

Figure 132

12 CH'ENG CHIANG

This area controls drinking and travelling by sea, since it rules the water. If the area is dark in the morning before you wash be careful what you drink; if you are travelling by ship, wait until the dark patch on the area disappears since you are in danger of sinking or drowning. A man who lacks hair on the *ch'eng chiang* has to be careful about what he eats and drinks in case it is poisonous. White, green or dark red skin on the *ch'eng chiang* denotes stomach problems when drinking or eating.

13 TI KO

The *ti ko* should be round, slightly upturned and strong in appearance. If you have these characteristics your old age will be extremely happy. A sharp, thin *ti ko* is unlucky: you may have a long life but there will be difficulties with money and friends (Figure 133). If the eyes and nose are badly proportioned and the *ti ko* slopes to the right or the left, you easily forget friendships and exact revenge against those who have offended you. You use

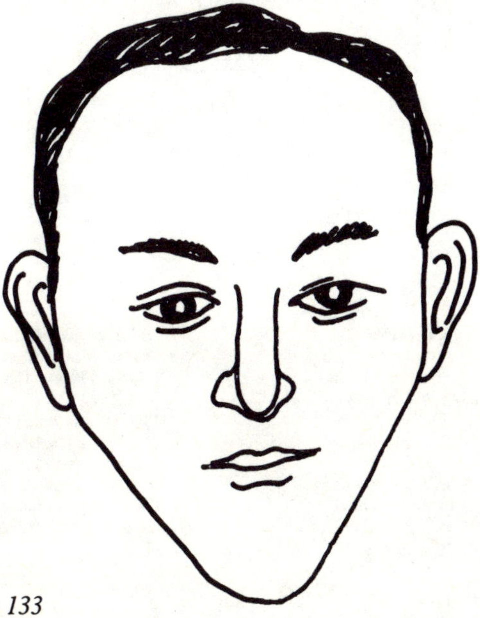

Figure 133

friends as the need arises and even disregard those who are close to you. If the *ti ko* is marked, scarred or cut, you do not have a family inheritance. A line running across the *ti ko* destroys its goodness, and dirty or smoky marks in this area signify a family sickness or an accident.

The Twelve Palaces of the Face

The Twelve Palaces are to be found in a variety of different areas of the face (Figure 134), as opposed to the Thirteen Positions which form a line down the centre.

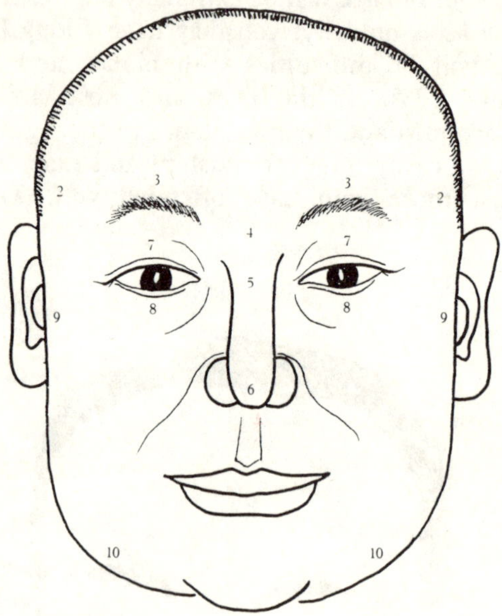

1 官祿宮 *Kuan Lu Kung* (Career Palace)
2 遷移宮 *Ch'en I Kung* (Movement Palace)
3 兄弟宮 *Hsiung Ti Kung* (Brothers' Palace)
4 命宮 *Min Kung* (Life Palace)
5 疾厄宮 *Chi O Kung* (Sickness Palace)
6 財帛宮 *Ts'ai Pai Kung* (Wealth Palace)
7 田宅宮 *T'ien Chai Kung* (House and Farm Palace)
8 男女宮 *Nan Nu Kung* (Man and Woman Palace)
9 妻妾宮 *Ch'i Ch'ien Kung* (Wife and Mistress Palace)
10 奴僕宮 *Nu P'u Kung* (Servant's Palace)
11 福德宮 *Fu Te Kung* (Fortune and Virtue Palace)
12 相貌宮 *Hsiang Mao Kung* (Face Palace)

Figure 134 The Twelve Palaces

1 KUAN LU KUNG (Career Palace)

The *kuan lu kung* is in the centre of the forehead. This area should not protrude or be too dome-shaped, and the complexion ought to be bright, clear and clean. These combined characteristics signify a famous person who will form strong friendships and can rely upon a respected and wealthy friend to help him in times of difficulty. An uneven forehead means lack of success or fame. Moles on the forehead also signify a difficult life.

2 CH'IEN I KUNG (Movement Palace)

This area ought to be well rounded and hollow. It signifies safety on a long journey and success in business. A sunken, dull *ch'ien i kung* warns against long journeys or emigration, since you are likely to lose your life or your possessions. A mole in this area is an indication that you should not move too far from home, since this could be dangerous.

3 HSIUNG TI KUNG (Brothers' Palace)

The brothers' palace refers to two types of brothers – those born of the same parents and those who are linked by friendship. If the eyebrows are longer than the eye, you have many real brothers, and if the eyebrows are well shaped and distinct, you are on very good terms with your family. Someone whose eyebrow is broken near the middle will argue with his brother. Eyebrows which are shorter than the eyes denote few brothers; and eyebrows which are long with unruly hairs signify family arguments. The Chinese say that the relationship between a man and his brothers is the highest relationship possible, and if you cannot treat your brothers well, what sort of treatment can your friends expect? The same reading will apply to women, although it may be hindered by the fact that women pluck their eyebrows.

4 MIN KUNG (Life Palace)

The *min kung* is the same position as the *yin t'ang* and reveals what the heart feels and thinks. If the *min kung* is wrinkled, you are in the midst of difficulties and are trying your utmost to sort them out. A bright, clear *min kung* is a sign of a fortunate life. This position relates to the heaven and human areas (see p. 115–18) and expresses the emotional side of our nature. A scarred or dull *min kung* is an indication of little success, even if the other features are well balanced. Good opportunities slip through your fingers. If this position has an unbroken line running through it, your life will be short or your death accidental. Somebody who dies unexpectedly may have always looked healthy but probably had a line running through the *min kung*.

Someone whose eyebrows are wide apart wastes his time on doomed plans. A wide *min kung* can also signify an inability to cope with money. Someone between the ages of twenty-five and thirty who lacks wrinkles in the *min kung* area rarely uses his brain and usually gives little or no consideration to any work he undertakes. He is, therefore, financially unsuccessful. It is normal to have at least two straight lines running down the length of the *min kung* by middle age.

5 CHI O KUNG (Sickness Palace)

This is the area between the *shou shang* and the *yin t'ang* and indicates whether you are poor, wealthy, healthy or ill. A rounded, smooth and wrinkle-free *chi o kung* is a sign of a strong mind, auspicious fortune and good health, but a flat *chi o kung* which is crossed by irregular lines or marked with a mole denotes bad luck. Friends will find your character difficult to deal with. A person with a badly formed *chi o kung* changes his mind quickly, is unsuccessful and will be prone to illness. The *chi o kung* can give accurate readings at the ages of twenty-six, thirty or forty-one.

6 TS'AI PAI KUNG (Wealth Palace)

This position is the same as the *chun t'ou* and is an indication of your economic standing. If the cheeks and the sides of the nose are flat, so that the nose is prominent, you will have difficulty making money and will lose any that you have. Since the nose has no support from the cheeks, the Chinese say that this is a 'lonesome hill'. The opposite will apply if your nose is supported by the lower cheeks. Your career will involve trading or merchant activities. Any marks or moles which can be seen when looking at the nose from directly in front are considered lucky. An accidental scar on the nose is a warning to take care around the age of forty-four, since you may have business trouble, family trouble, an accident or even a burglary during which you will be hurt. Natural marks on the skin are an indication that you will be responsible for your own misfortune.

7 T'IEN CHAI KUNG (House and Farm Palace)

This area predicts the happiness and success of your home and career. A *t'ien chai kung* which is clean, bright and free of dark patches denotes a comfortable lifestyle, pleasant job and peace of mind. You will have difficulty settling down at home or at work if the area is grey, smoky or scarred. Throughout life you will be discontented, and although you are wise you usually misjudge situations due to your lack of forethought. A mole or dark marks on the *t'ien chai kung* denote a dirty or untidy house and shabby or careless dressing. Someone with these features may also sense a strange or ghostly presence in his house. The position of the eyebrow will improve the reading. A high eyebrow is a lucky sign but if it is too high it denotes low intelligence.

8 NAN NU KUNG (Man and Woman Palace)

The area underneath the eyes is examined in order to predict happiness in family life. A clear, smooth unblemished *nan nu kung* is a sign of many children and strong parental love. Relationships amongst family and friends are kind and sincere. Lumpy, baggy or grey skin indicates few children, and those children will fall into trouble, thus causing many headaches for their parents. A mole in this area denotes childlessness and dishonest speech. In the words of the Chinese, 'The heart may say yes but the mouth says no.' Although the face may appear handsome, the thoughts are cunning and selfish. Crossing lines in the *nan nu kung* are a warning sign that this person is either childless or that his children will leave home at an early age, maintaining little or no contact. Prominent veins or dark skin colouring around the eyes denote too little sleep and too much time spent with a partner.

9 CH'I CH'IEN KUNG (Wife and Mistress Palace)

The Chinese use this area to determine whether a man or a woman is happy with his or her spouse. If the skin is soft and clear and the cheekbones do not protrude, you have a wise partner who offers help and support. Taut skin and thin muscle are indicative of marriage problems. A woman who has a badly formed *ch'i ch'ien kung* will want to commit adultery, or at least she will be incompatible with her husband.

Sometimes there are different patterns to the right and left of the face, so a man's reading is taken from the left-hand side and a woman's from the right. A man whose *ch'i ch'ien kung* is well formed on the right has a strong love for his wife, but if the skin is dented or taut he is likely to be dishonest or adulterous. If a woman's *ch'i ch'ien kung* is well formed on the left, she is honest, but if it is dented or marked, she will bring shame to her husband.

Accurate readings can be difficult due to the fact that some people are naturally thin and so their cheekbones protrude. An additional reading can be taken from the eye. Irregularly intertwined fishtail lines are also an indication of a quarrelsome relationship between husband and wife (Figure 135).

Figure 135

A man who has a mole on the right-hand side of his *ch'i ch'ien kung* is always in search of female relationships. At its worst he may be a rapist, referred to by the Chinese as a 'colour wolf'. A woman who has a mole on the left-hand side of the *ch'i ch'ien kung* takes great pleasure in male company but she does not have as cruel a nature as the colour wolf.

Marriage will be successful if the complexion of the *ch'i ch'ien kung* is bright, glossy and clean, but unstable and adulterous if this area is grey and dull.

10 NU P'U KUNG (Servants' Palace)

This area governs the ability of a person to form close friendships. Someone whose *nu p'u kung* is well rounded with a discernible shape has many good and honest friends. Those under his authority willingly obey his instructions. If the area is too thin, lacks muscle and the bone protrudes, you offend people who have helped you.

11 FU TE KUNG (Fortune and Virtue Palace)

There are no definite points to look for on the *fu te kung*. A reading should be taken from the facial expression, which usually reflects your emotions and personality.

12 HSIANG MAO KUNG (Face Palace)

A reading of the Face Palace is made by examining the features to check that the nose, mouth, eyebrows, eyes and ears are well balanced and harmonious. Any marks, dents or dull skin colouring will detract from the reading.

The Three Areas of the Face

The face is divided into three areas known as the heavenly, human and earthly areas (Figure 136). The heavenly area reaches from the hairline to just above the ears. The second area, known as the human, stretches down to the tip of the nose, and the third area, the earthly, stretches from the tip of the nose down to the chin. These three areas are referred

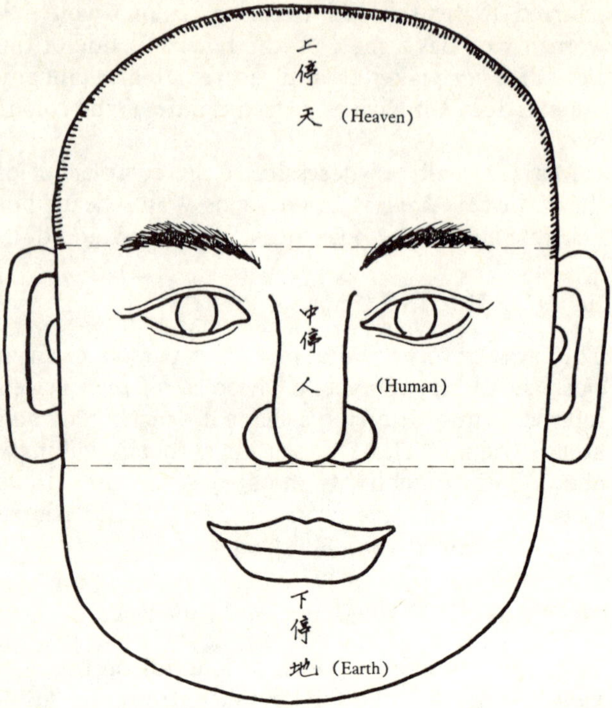

Figure 136 The Three Areas

to for readings in youth, middle age and old age respectively. Certain past and future events can be revealed by an examination of these areas.

THE HEAVENLY AREA

Well-developed features in the heavenly area denote good parents, strong education and concerned family support. A man ought to examine the left-hand side of his face to see whether it is scarred, dented or grey in colour; a woman ought to examine the right-hand side. Someone whose heaven area is badly formed will have many family difficulties and is likely to have had a poor or unhappy childhood.

A wide forehead is a fortunate feature, but if it is too wide it can detract from a good complexion or a good shape. This is particularly applicable to women

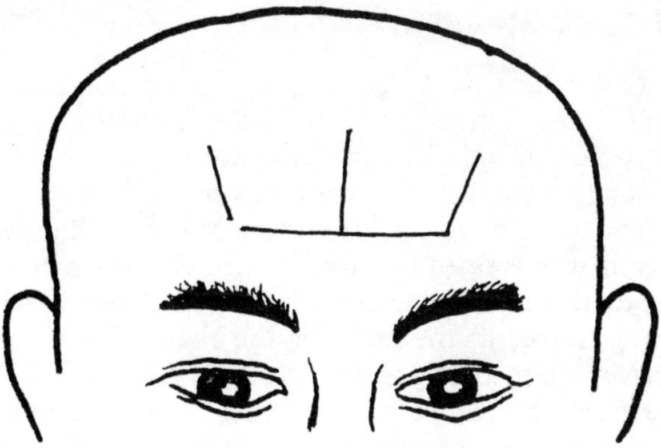

Figure 137

since it indicates marriage difficulties. Someone who reaches middle age ought to have at least three lines on the forehead, since this denotes thought before action, and expresses an understanding of human nature. A favourable reading will be given for forehead lines which curve upwards. If there are more than three lines or if the lines are broken and irregular, you will have troubles during your life. A man is likely to spend time away from his wife because of his business affairs. These lines are also indicative of an unstable family relationship. If your lines form the Chinese character for 'mountain' (山) (Figure 137) or for 'king' (王) (Figure 138), you will be rich and respected.

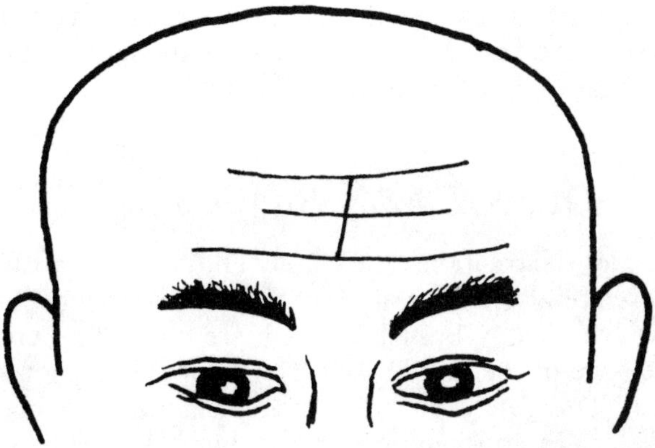

Figure 138

THE HUMAN AREA

A nose which has a harmonious appearance and is well balanced in relation to the other features is a sign of success in middle age. Irregular features signify unstable relationships during this time of life.

You have a strong, decisive mind if the human area is well formed and longer than the heavenly or the earthly areas. You are suited to disciplined jobs, for example, in the army or the police force, and derive enjoyment from adventurous work. A balanced human area combined with irregular features in the heavenly and earthly areas denotes dangerous events in life. Someone who has a dull complexion in the human area will be unsuccessful in business and cannot be trusted because he is involved in illegal activities.

THE EARTHLY AREA

A well-formed earthly area signifies a comfortable and happy old age. You will be respected by your children and grandchildren and will never be poor. Someone whose earthly area is unbalanced, thin, scarred or sharp will be unhappy, poor and lonely, and his children will not be concerned about his happiness during his final years.

A man whose earthly area is fat and who has thick lips will have many wives, but thin, pale-coloured lips denote weak health, even between the ages of twenty-five and thirty-five, the time thought by the Chinese to be the strongest period of life.

The Twelve Earthly Branches

Besides the positions, the palaces and the three areas, there are also twelve areas of the face known as the Twelve Earthly Branches which are marked around the edge of the face in a clockwise direction (Figure 139). The Twelve Earthly Branches are used to forecast health and happiness from the ages of seventy to one hundred years. In astrology each stem is

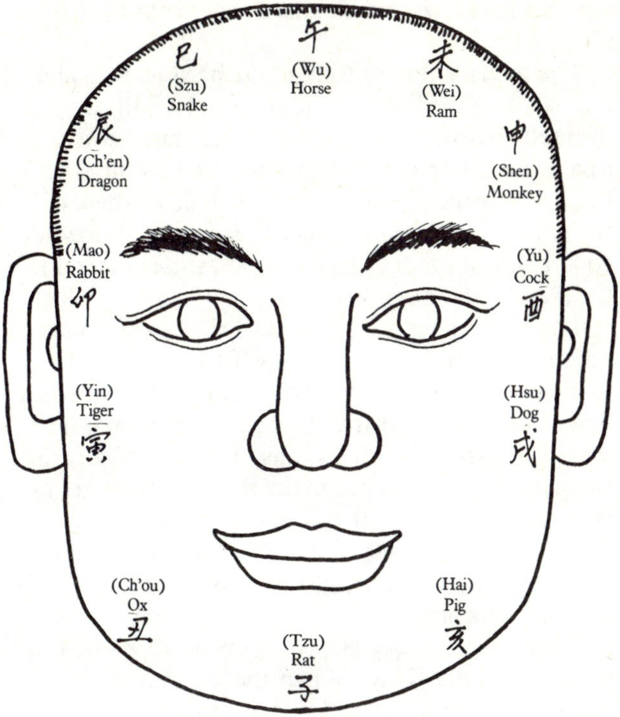

Figure 139 The Twelve Earthly Branches

represented by an animal, and Chinese legend relates how the Jade King, the god of heaven, chose them.

The Jade King and the Twelve Earthly Branches

The Jade King was extremely bored since he had so little to do; he was waited upon by his aides and servants, and because he lived in heaven he had no idea what happened on earth. In an effort to amuse himself he summoned his chief adviser. 'I have ruled for many years,' said the King, 'but I have never seen the animals on earth. What do they look like?' The adviser told him that there were many animals on earth. Did the Jade King wish to see them all? 'Oh no!' replied the King.

'I will waste so much time if I do that. Instead I want you to select the twelve most interesting animals and I will grade them according to their peculiarity.'

The adviser thought long and hard as to which animals might please the king. First of all he decided to send an invitation to the rat; he also asked the rat to pass on an invitation to his friend the cat. Further invitations were sent to the ox, tiger, rabbit, dragon, snake, horse, ram, monkey, cock and dog, telling them to be at the palace for six o'clock the next morning.

The rat was extremely proud to be summoned before the Jade King and set off to tell the cat their good news. The cat was delighted to hear the news but was afraid that he might oversleep; he therefore made the rat promise to wake him early the next morning. That night the rat pondered on how handsome the cat was and how ugly he would appear in comparison. The only way to prevent the cat taking the limelight was to let him oversleep the next morning.

Early the next day eleven animals were lined up before the Jade King. When the King reached the end of the line he turned to his adviser. 'They are all very interesting, but why are there only eleven?' The adviser had no answer, and for fear that the King would think he had not performed his task properly he sent a servant down to earth and ordered him to catch the first animal he found and bring it up to heaven. The servant arrived on a road and saw a man carrying a pig, and so he took the pig to the parade.

Meanwhile the rat was afraid that the King might not see him since he was so small; the only thing to do was to sit on the ox's back and play a flute. That way the King must notice him. The King did indeed notice him, and was so delighted with this unusual animal that he gave him first place. The Jade King gave the ox second place since he was kind enough to let the rat sit on his back. Since the tiger looked courageous he was given third place, and the rabbit, because of his fine white fur, was given fourth place. The King thought the dragon looked like a strong snake on legs, so he was given fifth place. The snake was given sixth place, the horse seventh, the ram eighth, the monkey ninth, the cock tenth (he was the only bird with wings which the adviser knew his servant could catch), and the dog was given eleventh place. The pig was ugly, but the King had no choice but to give him twelfth place.

After the awards ceremony had been performed the cat came dashing into the palace and begged the King to give him a chance. 'I'm sorry,' said the King. 'You are too late. I have arranged the Twelve Earthly Branches and I cannot go back on my choice.' On hearing this the cat was furious and went in search of the rat who had deceived him. When the cat spotted the rat he chased him with the intention of killing him. That is why, even today, a cat cannot be friends with a rat.

10
Additional Face Readings and the Three Areas of the Body

A full reading of the face is not limited to the positions dealt with in chapter 9, and includes an examination of what the Chinese refer to as the Five Mountains and Four Rivers. Other aspects which are checked during a full reading are hair, beard, voice and moles. The body, like the face, is also divided into three areas, and a general examination of bodily proportions, including the feet, will add to the physiognomist's final forecast.

THE FIVE MOUNTAINS (*Figure 140*)

The chin is known as the North Mountain, the forehead the South Mountain, the left cheek the East Mountain and the right cheek the West Mountain. The nose is the Central Mountain and acts as the commander of the face. If one of the mountains is sunken, hollow, damaged, weak or marked, particularly the West or East Mountains, then the Central Mountain lacks support. Someone with this feature cannot rely on others for help and will be successful only so long as he keeps his independent spirit. A woman whose forehead, the South Mountain, is smooth and well rounded, but disproportionate to the rest of her face, will marry seven times in quick succession. If her South Mountain is sharp and bony and her ears grow outwards she will have three marriages.

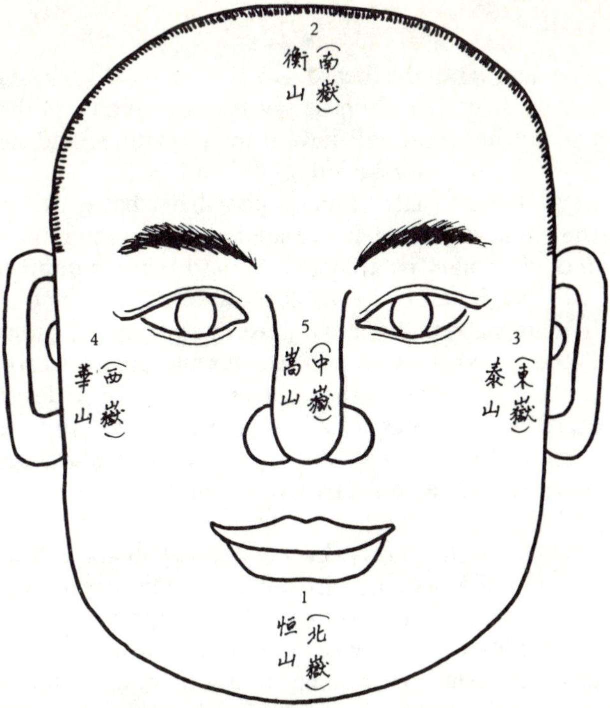

1 Heng Shan (North Mountain)
2 Heng Shan (South Mountain)
3 T'ai Shan (East Mountain)
4 Hua Shan (West Mountain)
5 Sung Shan (Central Mountain)

Figure 140 The Five Mountains

THE FOUR RIVERS

The ear is the Kong River, the eye the Ho River, the mouth the Wai River and the nose the Chai River. The Chinese say that the water of these rivers ought to be clear and clean. The *yan chung* is the important channel between the nose and the mouth which connects the four rivers. If the upper part of the *yan chung* is wider than the lower or if it is bent at some point, the flow of the river is hindered. The *yan chung* is not only concerned with family happiness but influences the characteristics which are controlled by the four rivers. So long as the rivers have a clear flow through this channel you will be lucky in business and in relationships.

HAIR

The hair and the beard are linked with luck and personality. The Chinese say that a woman who has hair on her chin will have a man's nature, and her marriage will not be successful unless her husband likes homosexuals. Thick, silky hair that grows in the same direction is considered lucky; thin, hard and wiry hair is unlucky. Smooth skin combined with rough hair or rough skin combined with smooth hair are signs that you will miss out on opportunities. Someone whose skin and hair texture are noticeably different will have a short life or an accidental death. Hard hair denotes a narrow-minded, hot-tempered person. Rough, dry, dull hair indicates a foolish, unfortunate person. His family will not respect him and his life is likely to be short.

Hair which is fairly thick and glossy in appearance is a sign of a patient, wise and fortunate person. The Chinese say that a woman's hair ought to be soft, reasonably thin and glossy. A woman who has hard, dry, rough hair may come from a rich family but in the end will be lonely and poor. A woman who has rough hair will not be satisfied with one husband.

Normally young people do not go grey, so someone under the age of thirty with white hair is overanxious. White hair can be expected after the age of forty. A man who still has a thick mane of dark hair at the age of sixty will have an unhappy relationship with his wife and children. He will not be poor, but will have few friends and little support from his family in his old age.

Someone who has growth points on the right- and left-hand sides of the scalp will always have to work hard to be successful. Someone whose hair grows from two circles on the centre of the head will be famous.

BEARD

The following comments on the beard also apply to moustaches and sideburns. The hair should not be too thick, too thin or too greasy. Hair which is dry and grows in different directions is a sign of problems in old age. A rough-looking beard indicates bad luck after middle age. The eyebrows give a fairly accurate reading from youth to early middle age, and the beard gives an accurate reading from late middle age to old age. A man who has a wispy beard has a weak character and cannot fulfil his promises.

VOICE

The quality of the voice has to be considered in relation to the sex of the person. A man who has a light, thin, fluting voice or a woman who has a deep, masculine voice will have an unlucky life and is likely to end up in a divorce court. A man should have a strong, loud voice, and a woman a soft, gentle voice. A man whose voice lacks undulation and sounds dry, and who gabbles when speaking will be unsuccessful in business. If a woman's voice is barely audible she will have troubles which cannot be solved easily, and will die young. The Chinese say that a woman with rough skin and a voice like the beating of a broken gong will end her life alone. The correct voice is rich and varied in tone, and clear and direct. Someone who has a loud, rough or croaking voice may have a successful business but will suffer economic difficulties. Even if the other features are well balanced the voice can detract from a good reading.

MOLES

Moles are not the most important aspect in physiognomy, but they do affect a reading. They are usually red, grey, light black or dark black. Red or black moles are lucky, but grey or light black moles are unlucky.

Moles can be found on any one of the thirteen positions (Figure 141). A mole on the *t'ien chung* is a sign of an argumentative relationship with parents (Figure 141 – a). Someone who has an unlucky mole on the *t'ien t'ing* (Figure 141 – b) or the *ssu k'ung* (Figure 141 – c) has been little influenced by his parents and since he did not heed their advice may

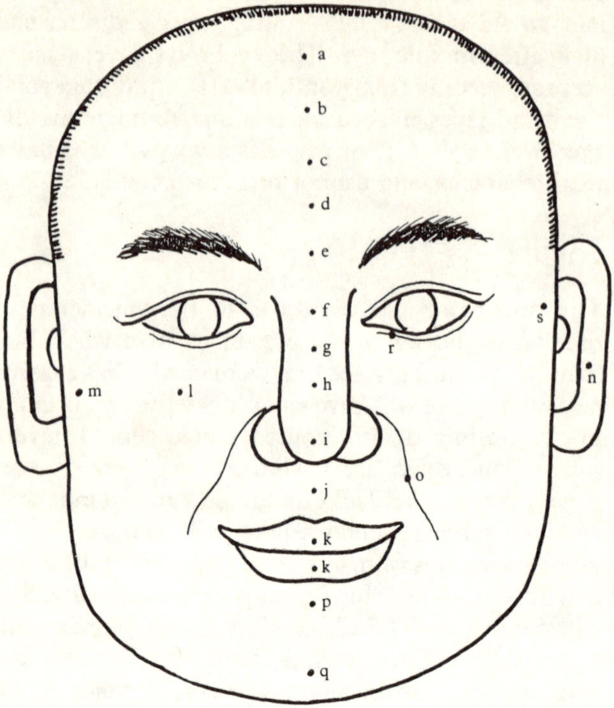

Figure 141

become involved in an accident connected with fire. This is true for men and women. A woman who has a mole in this position works very hard for her husband. A mole on the *chung cheng* (Figure 141 – d) is the sign of impatience.

A mole on the *yin t'ang* (Figure 141 – e) signifies a weak will, a gullible nature and a lack of thoroughness. Someone with a mole on the *shan ken* argues with his wife and will probably marry a second time. The same reading can be given for a woman. A mole in the centre of the *shan ken* (Figure 14 – f) denotes death in an accident.

A mole on the *nien shang* (Figure 141 – g) or *shou shang* (Figure 141 – h) signifies weak health and lack of money. A man who has a lightish mole in either of these areas will end up in confrontation in his relationships with women, whereas a woman with this mole will be misused by men. A lighter-coloured mole on the *chun t'ou* (Figure 141 – i) is a sign of financial loss, particularly through gambling. The Chinese refer to this as the 'capacity to destroy money'. A man who has a mole on the *chun t'ou* enjoys relationships with women, but will always have difficulties with his partner. A woman who has a mole in this area will work very hard for her husband although he is hot-tempered and selfish.

A man who has a lighter-coloured mole in the *jen chung* (Figure 141 – j) cannot enjoy his money, has unhelpful children and will die young. The same will apply for a woman, and in addition she may have gynaecological problems. A woman who has a line across the *jen chung* has committed adultery. Lighter-coloured moles are signs of a hospitable nature although there will be friendship difficulties due to awkwardness and selfishness.

A mole on the lips, the *shui hsing* (Figure 141 – k) is a good sign, since it denotes a healthy appetite both for food and for life. A mole on the palate is a sign of bad relationships with your children. If the mole appears on a wide palate a man will have more than one wife, and a woman is likely to take a lover in addition to her husband.

Someone who has a mole on the cheekbone (Figure 141 – l) is unlikely to be promoted. A mole in front of the ear signifies an accident involving fire (Figure 141 – m); one on any part of the ear implies an obedient and respectful nature (Figure 141 – n). A mole on the *fa ling* denotes a serious disaster or accident between fifty-six and fifty-seven years of age (Figure 141 – o). A mole on the *chien chiang* (Figure 141 – p) signifies death by drowning or poison, especially around fifty-four years of age. A mole on the *ti ko* is an indication of adoption and a difficult childhood. Someone who has a mole on the *ti ko* may have been brought up by relatives since his parents could not afford to keep him. It is also a sign of no family inheritance (Figure 141 – q).

A mole on the inside of the eye signifies enjoyment of male companionship. A mole in the area underneath the eye is a sign of difficulties with children (Figure 141 – r). Someone who has such a mole wants to spend time with his children but gets little opportunity to do so. A mole on the wife and mistress palace is an indication of a lover or more than one marriage (Figure 141 – s).

THE COMPLEXION

The complexion is difficult to read, and before doing so it is necessary to have a good understanding of physiognomy. The Chinese distinguish an energy flow, which is called *ch'i*. Someone with strong *ch'i* has good colouring since the *ch'i* has pushed the blood to the surface. A sick person has a pale face since he has weak *ch'i*. A correct reading cannot be made after physical exertion because the body will have pushed blood to the surface of the skin. When examining the complexion do not sit in strong light since this gives an inaccurate reading. The light must be soft and there should be no reflections from sunshine or strong spotlights. The colour of the complexion can vary from red, purple, green, yellow and deep red to white, black or grey.

Red is a happy colour and can signify a contented love life. Purple also indicates good luck and success. Green can be interpreted as fear or anger, and yellow signifies good news or money. A deep red denotes a disaster or an accident, possibly prosecution, jail, fire risk or physical injury. White is interpreted as worry or death, and black is a sign of sickness or loss of money. Someone who has a grey colouring wastes time and is therefore likely to fail in business or lose money.

The luckiest colours are red, purple and yellow. If these colours are dull you are lacking true energy flow; this could be because bad luck is at hand in the form of an accident or a disaster. Unlucky colours are white, green, black or a very deep red. However, someone with one of these colours may be lucky if his face appears bright and alert. This is an indication of forthcoming good fortune. Whatever colour the face may be, the skin should be moist, bright and full of *ch'i*, and the expression animated. An unevenly coloured complexion is an unlucky feature, known by the Chinese as a 'false complexion'.

The Monk and the Tea Boy

High in the mountains of China there lived a monk who was a teacher of physiognomy. He was helped in his daily tasks by a young tea boy who had been living with him for several years. Many people came to consult the monk and paid him whatever they could afford: he even read the fortunes of those who could not pay. One morning the monk noticed a sudden change in the boy's complexion, which had become dull and sallow. He decided to calculate what this could mean and so he asked the boy to give him the piece of paper upon which his mother had written the time and day of his birth.

For many hours the monk repeated his calculations by examining the tea boy's physiognomy and reading his hand, but he always came up with the same result: the boy would die within ten days. The monk did not reveal this frightening prediction to the boy; he simply told him to gather his personal belongings and return to his family home so that he could be with those closest to him before his death. The tea boy begged his master to tell him what he had done wrong, but the wise fortune-teller would not give an explanation.

A month passed and the tea boy was still alive and well. His parents now told him to return to his master since the monk was sure to need the tea boy's help. He gathered his belongings and set off towards the monk's house, high in the mountains. The monk heard footsteps and looked up from his book: to his amazement he saw the tea boy standing in front of him. He couldn't understand why the boy had returned and reasoned that his calculations must have been wrong. After examining the boy again he still had the same result, the tea boy must die soon.

The monk was both excited and scared, and demanded to be told exactly what had happened on the tea boy's journey to his parents' home. The tea boy told him how he had left on a very hot day, so hot that he had to rest by a mountain stream. When he looked down he saw many ants clambering around an ant hill at the side of the stream. The tea boy realized that a heavy rain would swell the stream to such an extent that it would destroy the ant hill. As a means of protection he built a wall of sand and stones around the ants; he then took off his underwear and bound it around the wall to act as an additional safeguard.

The monk listened carefully to the tea boy's story and then he spoke: 'You were definitely going to die, but because you saved the lives of so many ants you were granted life in return.'

The Three Areas of the Body

As the face is divided into three areas, so is the body. The area from the head to the shoulders is known as the heavenly area, that from the shoulders to the waist as the human area, and that from the waist to the toes as the earthly area. The best reading is obtained when all three areas are well balanced. A well-proportioned body does not depend on height – you can judge whether your body is in proportion, no matter what its height. A badly proportioned body detracts from the good reading obtained from a balanced face. If you have well-formed heavenly and human areas, but thin, weak legs and a flat bottom, then you have an unlucky physiognomy; you will be successful in business but will lose all your money in old age. The Chinese say that the heavenly and human areas combined should always appear longer than the legs.

The Feet

The feet have to carry the weight of the whole body, and during their life they will walk many hundreds of miles. An examination of the feet can reveal whether you are poor and lowly or rich and noble.

The ideal foot should be square-shaped, wide and long, and the skin should be soft. The feet should not be flat or turn outwards or inwards. Such a foot is a sign of a rich and noble person. The foot of a poor or lowly person is thin and short, and the skin feels rough. Thick, wide feet or very long, narrow feet signify a difficult life.

A foot with no obvious lines on the sole is unlucky, but many lines denote healthy eating and drinking. Eye-shaped lines on the soles of the feet signify good fortune for your children and grandchildren. Circular lines indicate fame, and a tortoiseshell pattern is a sign of a prosperous life. The luckiest toes are those which are soft and well formed.

11
Animal Shapes

The body can be read in relation to the Five Elements or in relation to animal shapes. Frequently someone may remind us of a certain animal because of his features or the way he moves, speaks or eats. It may seem strange that someone with an odd appearance and an unbalanced physiognomy should be lucky in life but the Chinese say that a resemblance to an animal bestows particular qualities on an individual. Below are the main animal shapes which are listed in ancient Chinese physiognomy.

PHOENIX SHAPE

The eyes are long and narrow and there is no eyelid. The eyes are clear, the nose curved, the lower cheeks and chin narrow. The body is long and slight. The voice is clear, the walk elegant.

You have an alert character and are endowed with a gentle, creative nature. Whether you are male or female you will be well respected. You are likely to attain a high official rank.

EAGLE SHAPE

The head is square, with a wide, round forehead. The eyebrows are thick, the eyes bright and round with tinges of yellow and red in the iris. The mouth is small, the lips full and pursed. The ears are at a high level.

You respond quickly, with decisive and forceful actions. By nature you like to kill and are suited to a job involving combat – a good example might be a soldier. You are generally respected and successful but will not have a quiet or gentle death.

CRANE SHAPE

Prominent cheekbones, downward sloping eyebrows, narrow cheeks and chin, with hollows under the cheeks. The nose is sharp, thin and high, and the neck thin and long. Although the body is thin, when walking the stride is wide.

By nature you are clever and will attain a good position in your career, but you will not choose fame and fortune as you derive greater pleasure from a peaceful, quiet life.

GOOSE SHAPE

The mouth and eyes are small and the nose turns inwards at the tip; the body is long but the legs short. Although movements are slow they are regulated so that each task is performed gradually, step by step.

You are content with your life and have a comfortable and comparatively rich lifestyle.

MAGPIE SHAPE

A small face, with high-placed ears and a greenish-white tinge to the skin. The walk is quick, the voice clear. Such a person chooses his words meticulously.

You are respected for your wisdom and knowledge and people enjoy listening to you speak. Although you will never be rich you will be happy.

DUCK SHAPE

A round body, short legs and a small mouth. The walk is very slow.

You are not considered beautiful or handsome but have a pleasant character and can make friends easily. You are lucky, enjoy good health and have a strong stomach for eating and drinking.

PIGEON SHAPE

Small stature, with a white face and greenish-red eyes.

You are fond of singing and humming to yourself and can never sit still for long. Domestic problems do not worry you but you will never be successful unless you set up in a business partnership.

PARTRIDGE SHAPE

Red skin colouring; the iris is marked with red and yellow tinges and the body and ears are small. Such a person looks at the floor when walking, and his head moves from side to side.

You will struggle to earn a decent living, and do not derive much pleasure from life.

MANDARIN-DUCK SHAPE

Pinkish face and round eyes slightly upturned at the corner. This person's footsteps are uneven in length and his walk is usually jerky.

You consider your movements but have a tendency to use bad language. Like most mandarin-duck-shaped people, you are interested in the opposite sex and like to flirt if the opportunity arises. You depend on friends if there are any domestic problems and will be quite wealthy if you have good *ch'i*.

CROW SHAPE

A round face, large nose, pursed lips and dark eyes with a hint of green.

Once you start to talk you are loathe to stop although nobody really wants to listen to you. By nature you are greedy; you will never be rich.

DRAGON SHAPE

The Five Mountains are rounded and well formed, the body large-boned, and powerfully built. Clear eyes and thick eyebrows which rise upwards. The walk is determined and steady, and the face straight and reliable; such a person does not easily break into laughter.

The true dragon-shaped person can be trusted since his thoughts are worthy and honest. This particular shape is rarely seen and is believed to be the physiognomy of a holy man, distinguished by wealth and nobility.

TIGER SHAPE

There are four kinds of tiger shape:

Forest Tiger
The first type has a large head, thickset back, and strong shoulders. The back of the neck is square, the waist round, the forehead high and the lips deep red. The eyes are large, clear and bright.

You will immediately sense that this type of person has a powerful physical presence which is combined with a strong, clear voice. His behaviour is calm and controlled. He will usually attain a high position in government or the armed services.

Out-of-the-Forest Tiger
The body shape is the same as that of the forest tiger, the only difference being that this type glances quickly from side to side and usually looks upwards when he walks.

You will be respected and rich but will not hold on to your wealth for very long.

Mountain Tiger
The third type has the same build as the tiger-shaped person but his behaviour and actions are less certain since he is always preoccupied with other matters.

You may be rich or poor, but you are usually prone to bad luck rather than good fortune.

Crossing-the-Mountain Tiger
The final type also has a tiger build, but his face is worried and alert.

Although you often look ill, you are, in fact, quite healthy. You are rich and respected but troubled by many worries. At some time in your life you may be very wealthy, but will die soon after acquiring this fortune.

LION SHAPE

A square head, high forehead, large nose and eyes. The iris and pupil ought to be clear and bright and the bones at the back of the head are well developed. The Chinese call this area the 'pillow stone' since it is the first part of the head to touch the pillow. The hair is thick and strong.

Others look to you for guidance, and you will be well respected and rich.

ELEPHANT SHAPE

A wide forehead, high eyebrows which grow beyond the eye tail, and large ears which lack rings or wheels. The nose is upturned and the lips curl outward so that the teeth can be seen. This type is well built with strong muscles and whenever he moves his actions are deliberate and steady.

Kindness and generosity come naturally to you and you are respected and rich.

GIBBON SHAPE

The face and features are round and small, the lips pursed, the voice loud; the arms are longer than the legs. Although the body is thin, the cheeks and chin are quite fat.

You have a sensitive nature but are quite vain and take pleasure in preening yourself in a mirror. Your actions are swift and monkey-like and you enjoy eating fruit and cleaning yourself. You are not suited to a creative career and can usually be found in a disciplined, orderly job. Although you are well known you will not be wealthy and are likely to have an unlucky old age.

MONKEY SHAPE

High cheekbones and round, deep-set eyes. The nose and ears are positioned high on the face and the complexion is tinged with yellow and red. Although the gestures tend to be unsteady, the movements are lively and unpredictable.

You are not courageous but you are extremely sensitive. You will have a comfortable life but will never be wealthy.

TORTOISE SHAPE

A dome-shaped head, round eyes, high nose, thick eyebrows, round jaw, long neck and thick shoulders. The body is quite fat and round and the Five Mountains of the face are well balanced.

Your disposition is calm and your life will be comfortable and rich.

SNAKE SHAPE

A narrow forehead, small eyebrows and a short, sharp nose. The eyes are long in shape and muddy green in colour; the lips are usually pursed and the teeth sharp. The ears are small and shaped like a question mark – wide at the top, narrow at the bottom and lacking a pearl. The waist is wide and the flesh feels soft. When walking there is a tendency to zigzag rather than go in a straight line.

Whether you are involved in good or bad deeds, you maintain secrecy, but your intentions are usually cruel whether they concern friends or family. You will die young.

COW SHAPE

A strong body, large head and powerful neck. The iris is large, black and bright. The mouth is large and the lips move even though the owner is not speaking. The walk is very slow.

You are kind by nature and are likely to be rich.

HORSE SHAPE

A long body and face, large eyes and mouth, and wide, strong teeth. The actions are slow and steady whether walking or sitting.

You are respected and rich and your whole life will be peaceful and calm.

LAMB SHAPE

A long face but the forehead cannot be seen clearly because it is either covered by hair or narrow in shape. The chin is thin and the lips are pursed. A lamb-shaped man is likely to have a small beard. The eyes are muddy yellow and the iris is small. The legs are quite short. When walking this type looks down at the floor.

The lamb-shaped man is well respected: the lamb-shaped woman is rich and enjoys flirting with men.

PIG SHAPE

A large head, long face, flat forehead, deep-set eyes, pursed lips, pointed ears, plump cheeks and short neck and legs.

You dress as though you are wealthy; in fact, you have no savings and are generally considered foolish. You should take care since you may die in an accident.

RAT SHAPE

Deep red complexion and round eyes. The rat-shaped person likes to stand in the shadows, cautiously watching other people, and even eats his food in secret in case anyone should see him.

You have a sensitive, cautious nature but will never be rich; you will only earn enough to support yourself. Unfortunately, you will have a tragic death.

RABBIT SHAPE

Small legs, head, eyebrow, forehead and mouth. The nose is slightly red and the ears large and rounded. There are many teeth which grow close together.

You will be respected and comparatively rich.

CAMEL SHAPE

A round head, long face, wide forehead, long neck, thick hair and rough eyebrows. The eye are thickset and the mouth pursed. Although the shoulders are rounded they are powerful, as are the arms and legs. The voice is loud and resonant.

You can be trusted to deliver a message or help those in need. You will be rich and respected.

A basic description has been given of the main types of animal shape, and although there are others, such as the lobster, fish or prawn, they are not easy to describe. Unless someone has obvious features or characteristics he cannot easily be put into one of the animal groups. In the end the most accurate way of reading someone's fortune is through traditional physiognomy and palmistry.

12
The Hands

The Relationship between Physiognomy and Palmistry

When the features of the face do not appear well balanced or harmonious it is best to make an examination of the hands to collect further information. If the features on the hand are better formed than those of the face, they can improve what would otherwise be an unlucky reading. The lines on the hand take longer to develop than the lines on the face and are more permanent; therefore they give a more accurate reading than the features of the face. Weak hand lines combined with weak facial lines and features signify bad luck, but weak facial features combined with deep, clear hand lines improve the reading considerably since the hand lines are still changing and growing.

A man's left hand and a woman's right hand reflect their own actions, thoughts, aspirations and fortune, whereas the opposite hand is the one influenced by our family and inherited characteristics. This hand is the one we are born with, whereas the other hand is the one we guide and alter. Each hand has its own responsibilities and does not control the other.

The six most important lines on the hand are the life line, the head line, the heart line, the career line, the success line, which helps the career line, and the marriage line (Figure 142). The three most important are the head, heart and life lines; the others are subordinate. On average there are thirty lines in the hand, although it is sufficient to take a reading from the six major lines.

There are also many different features on the lines, most of which are easily distinguished and which have special names, such as 'star', 'island', 'chain' and 'mountain'. An island is a round or oval-shaped

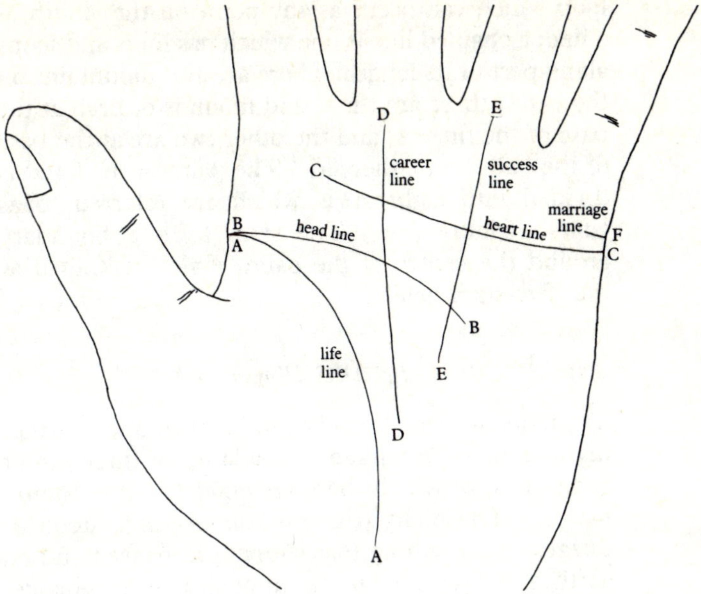

Figure 142

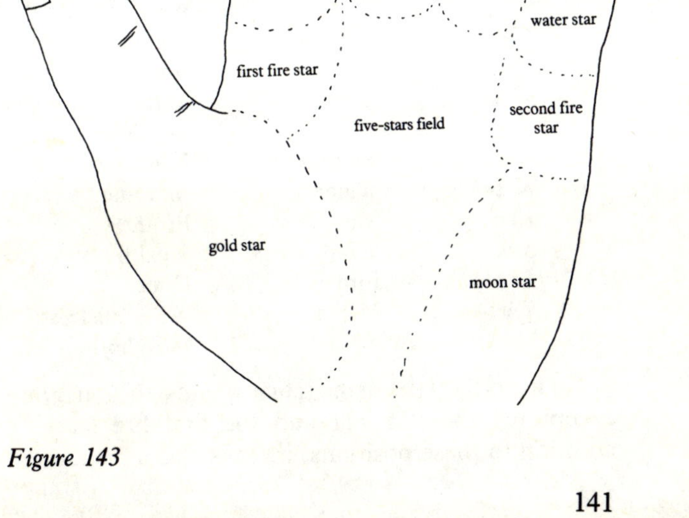

Figure 143

loop which can occur at any point on the length of a line; a chained line is one which has links and loops along part of its length. There are also mountains on the hand; three are the round mounds of flesh at the base of the fingers, and the other two are at the base of the palm, on either side. The palm of the hand is divided into eight areas which are referred to as 'stars' (Figure 143). The stars form a boundary around the centre of the palm, which is known as the 'five-stars field'.

The Eight Trigrams *(Figure 144)*

Trigrams are traditionally used in Chinese oracular divination. Each trigram is made up of three yin or yang lines, of which there are eight possible combinations. The eight trigrams can be understood as images of everything that happens in heaven and on earth and they are in a continual state of change, just as everything in our lives is constantly changing. When two trigrams combine together they form a hexagram of six yang or yin lines. There are sixty-four hexagrams which together form the ancient Chinese classic of divination, the *I Ching*.
Each trigram has a particular image and traditional meaning in Chinese physiognomy.

Trigram	*Image*	*Meaning in physiognomy*
Ch'ien	Heaven	Father and elder son
K'un	Earth	Mother and elder daughter
Chen	Thunder	Education
K'an	Water	Inheritance
Ken	Mountain	Brothers
Sun	Wind, wood	Wealth
Li	Fire	Fame
Tui	Marsh	Wife, mistress and children

Each star of the hand corresponds to a trigram except for the sun star and the first fire star. In addition to these positions, there is also a trigram on

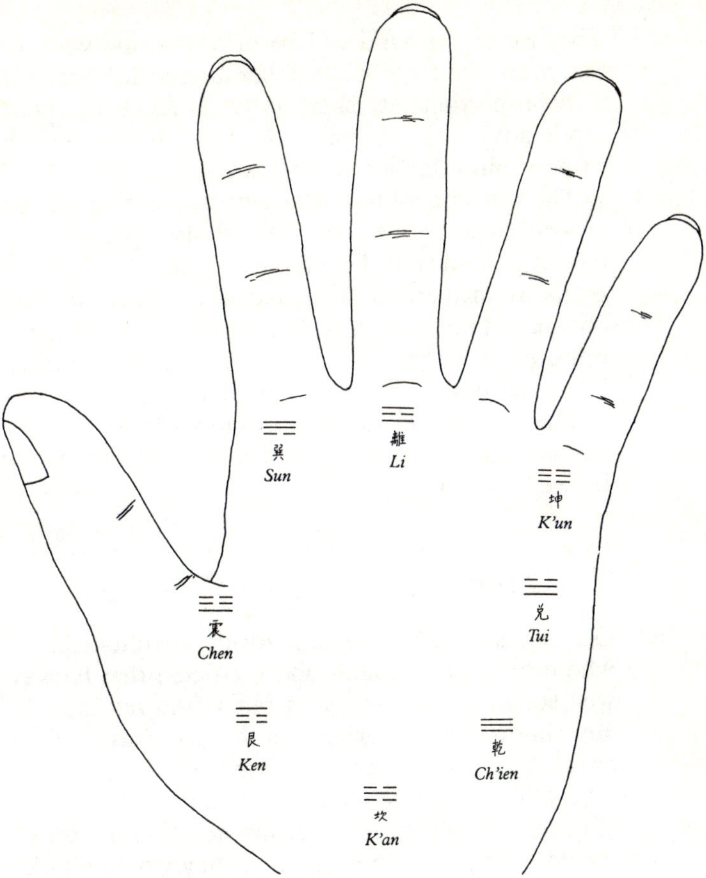

Figure 144 The Eight Trigrams

the lower middle palm which is known as *K'an*. The gold star has two trigrams – *Chen* and *Ken*. The *Sun* trigram is in the position of the wood star, the *Li* trigram is in the earth star, the *K'un* trigram in the water star, the *Tui* trigram in the second fire star and the *Ch'ien* trigram is in the moon star.

Success in each aspect of one's life will be determined by the growth pattern, shape and colour of the relevant area. It is an unlucky sign if these areas are too lined or too flat. Three horizontal lines below *K'an* are known as 'three-star line' and refer to fortune, career and long life.

The Perfect Hand

The size of the hand will be in proportion with the body; an overlarge hand is considered luckier than a disproportionately smaller hand. Since the brain sends advice to the hand, the hand has to assume responsibility for its owner's actions.

The skin should have elasticity and not be too soft or smooth since this is the sign of a lazy person. You have a good facility for making money if your hand is hard, strong, elastic, and the bones are not obvious. The skin should have good *ch'i* which is reflected in bright pinky red or yellow colouring. Dry grey skin is considered unlucky.

The fingers and the thumb should be strong and straight and the five mountains of the hand should be well rounded.

The Man with Thirteen Children

One day a man went by a roadside fortune-teller who examined his hands and predicted that he was well suited to moneymaking but would not have any children. On hearing this the man was completely shocked and informed the fortune-teller, 'You must be wrong, I have thirteen children.' The fortune-teller insisted that the man would have no children because they would all die within the year. The following year was a thirteen-month lunar year and, just as the fortune-teller had predicted, a child died each month.

The Shape and Feel of the Hand

A thick, soft hand and a powerful thumb signify long life (but this should be checked with the life line). The opposite will apply if the thumb is weak and the hand thin and too soft. A short, stumpy thumb and a badly shaped hand must be checked against the hand line before a definite conclusion is drawn, but even then a long life cannot be guaranteed. It is important to check whether the thumb is active or whether it just hands loosely, since this determines the owner's level of intelligence. The Chinese use the gorilla's hand as a comparison: it may have well-formed lines but its thumb hangs loosely at its side; although it is a strong animal it is not highly intelligent. The thumb is important in writing, drawing and manual work, and without its help the grip is weakened.

The Main Lines

The head, heart and life lines are the most important lines and ought to be unblemished and clear. The life line in particular ought to be long. The luckiest lines are not short, chained, grey nor interrupted by many cross lines or islands; they should be neither too deep nor too wide. The head line is the most important of the three and should be undamaged. In order to calculate to which age the markings on the lines refer the Chinese break the life line (Figure 145) and the heart and head lines (Figure 146) into age areas.

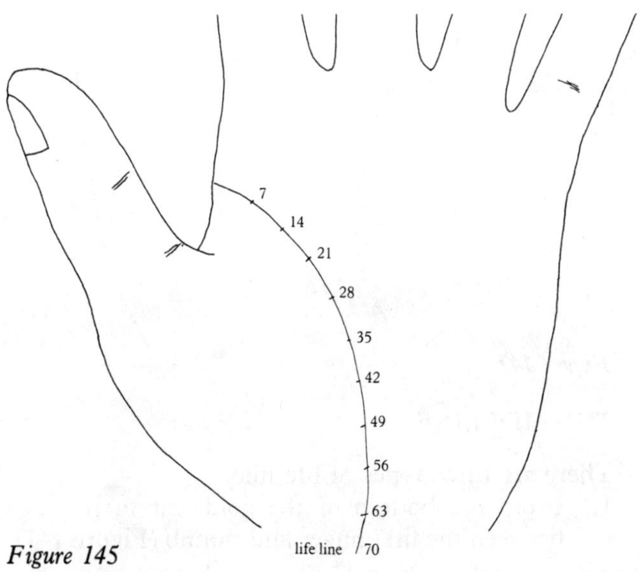

Figure 145

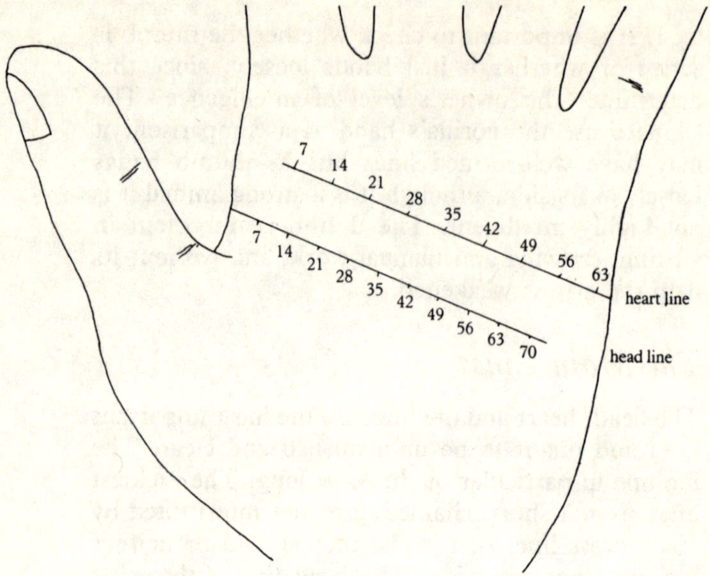

Figure 146

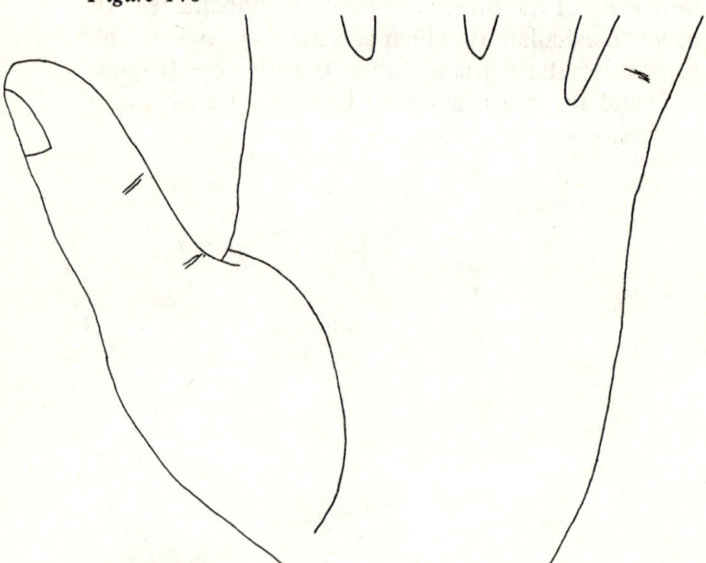

Figure 147

THE LIFE LINE

There are three types of life line:

1. From the bottom of the gold star to the area between the first finger and thumb (Figure 147).

2. From the middle of the hand to the area between the first finger and thumb (Figure 148).
3. From the moon star to the area between the first finger and thumb (Figure 149).

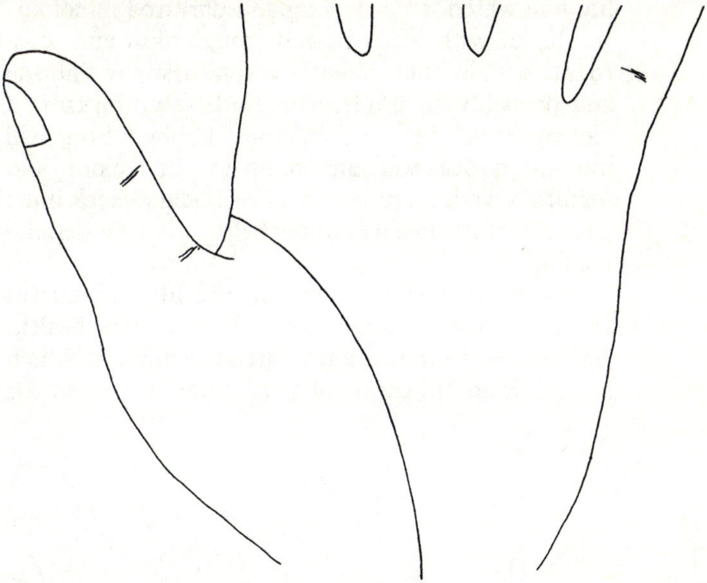

Figure 148

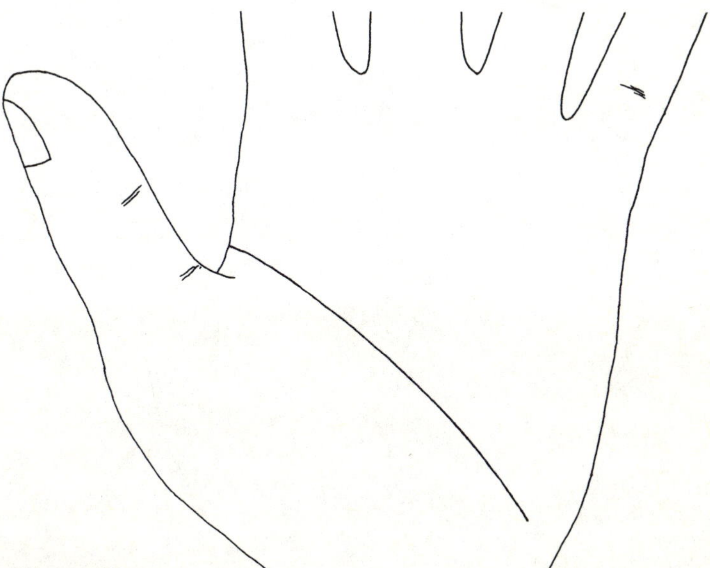

Figure 149

If any part of the life line is uneven, crossed or faint, then it is known as a rough line, and if the hand is grey in colour, you may have a strong build and quick reactions, but will not have a long life. A life line which is deep, long and dark red in colour, combined with a hard hand, rough skin and well-rounded gold star, denotes a fondness for fighting and probably an unpleasant death resulting from a violent attack or a dangerous hobby. You will initially notice warning signs in the colour and texture of your complexion. A secondary check must be made of the facial features before giving a definite reading.

If your gold star is flat and the life line curves around its bottom edge, you will have weak health. This is also an indication of greed. A life line which is weak is an indication of a short life, no matter the

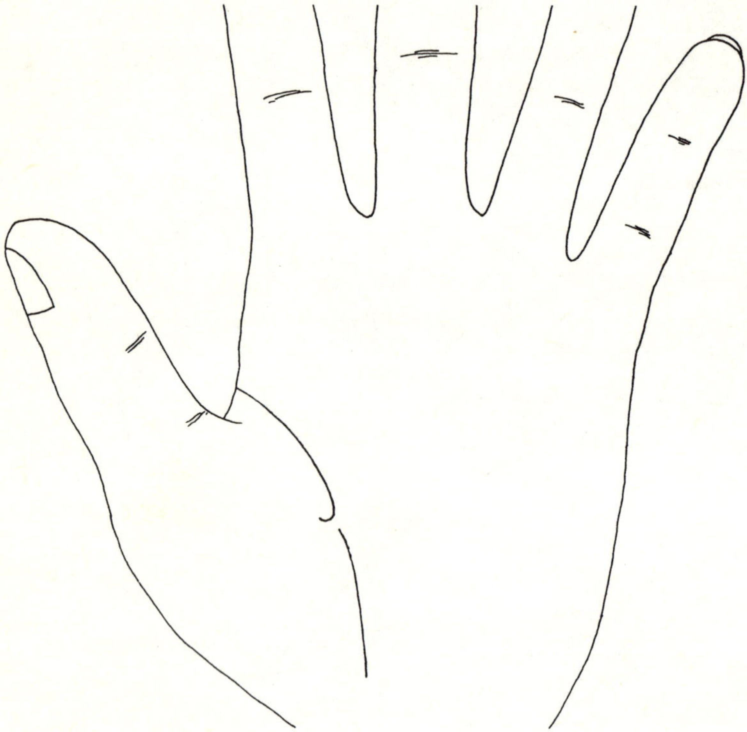

Figure 150

length of the line itself, but this can be improved if the thumb is straight, the hand thick and hard, and the head line clear and strong. Someone who has no life line or a very short life line may live to a great age but will suffer serious sickness or face dangerous risks. However, it is important to remember that a weak feature will be helped by strong ones.

The life line should not be broken at any part of its length. A life line which is hooked on both hands (Figure 150) signifies death during the year at which the line breaks away. If one line is straight but the other broken, then a serious illness or disaster will befall you. Two broken life lines (Figure 151) indicate a serious accident but not death, since help will arrive in time. But if these lines occur in combination with soft, thin hands, this accident will result in death.

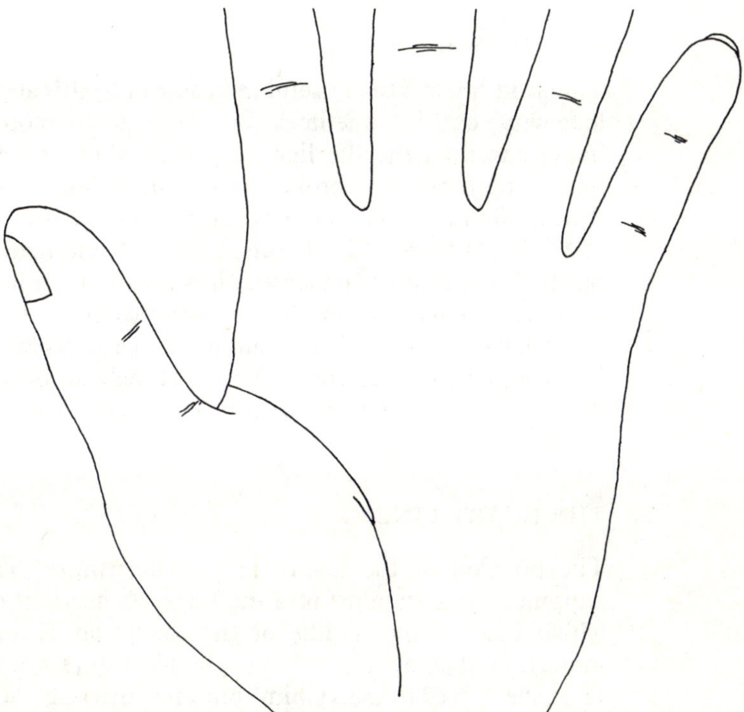

Figure 151

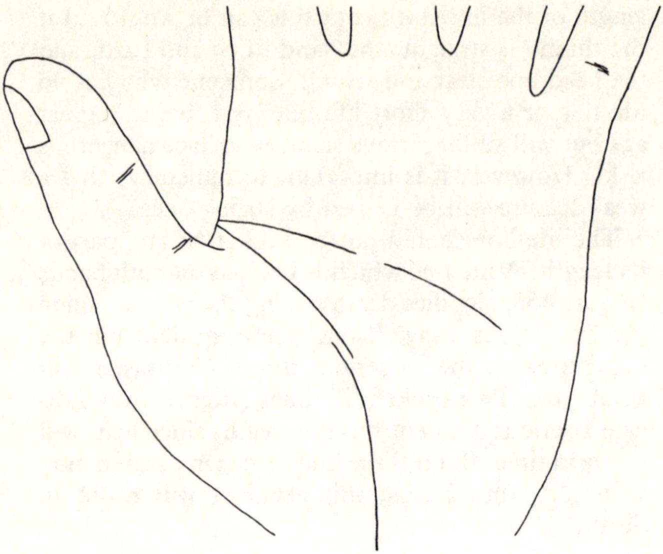

Figure 152

THE HEAD LINE

The head line is also a useful indicator of health and longevity, and is sometimes considered to be more important than the life line. Someone whose head line on both hands is broken at a point in line with the middle finger will die between the ages of thirty and forty (Figure 152). If this occurs on one hand but both the thumbs are strong, it is a sign of a head wound or mental problems between the ages of thirty and forty. Someone whose main hand line is broken but has a square in the gap will be helped by a wealthy and influential friend when faced with danger.

THE HEART LINE

The position of the heart line can determine the happiness and stability of a marriage. A heart line which reaches the middle of the earth star is an indication that a man will pursue his future wife until she agrees to marry him, but after marriage he will develop a strong possessive streak thus denying his wife independence (Figure 153). If the heart line grows from a point between the first and second finger, between the wood and the earth stars, the husband is not interested in his wife's previous history; the only important thing is that their love is strong and sincere (Figure 154 – a). A heart line which grows to the wood star means your love for your partner is honest and powerful, and is sure to be reciprocated (Figure 154 – b).

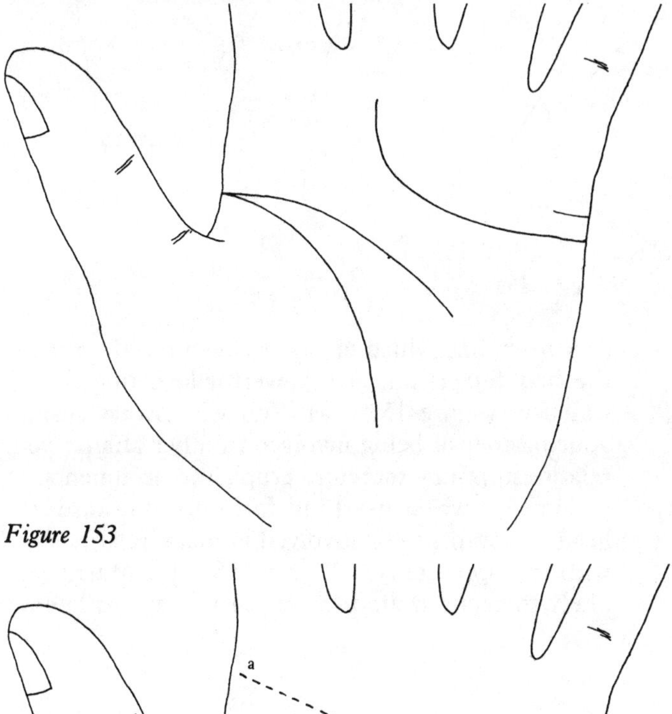

Figure 153

Figure 154

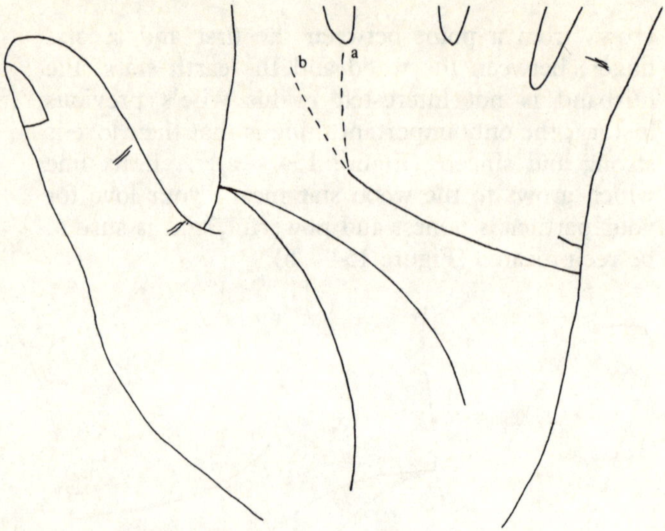

Figure 155

A heart line which grows between the thumb and the first finger indicates powerful love tinged with jealousy (Figure 155 – a). You will always suspect your partner of being involved in other affairs; your relationship may therefore erupt into arguments.

Someone whose heart line forks down towards the head line wants to be involved in many relationships with the opposite sex (Figure 155 – b). Marriage is likely to occur around thirty years of age or later.

13
The Hands: Career, Success and Marriage Lines

Badly formed head, heart and life lines and clear, unblemished career and success lines can be likened to a reservoir without a source or a tree without a root. Both success and career will be short-lived since the strong foundations are missing. The hand shape and the three main lines are the foundations and walls of the house and the career and success lines are the roof. A good hand shape combined with well-formed lines indicates a successful career with many useful and welcome opportunities. If the career line is strong but the success line is missing you will be reasonably successful but not particularly wealthy or well known. A bad reading will be given if the success line is missing and the career line is rough and grey or white in colour; you may work hard but earn little. Someone whose career, success and marriage lines are clear and well formed will have an above average standard of living. A woman who has a combination of faint and indistinct head, heart, life and career lines will probably be a widow or very unsettled in her life. The situation will be much improved if the success line is well formed.

THE CAREER LINE

A career line which begins at the base of the wrist and stops in the middle of the hand (Figure 156 – AA) is a sign of a difficult childhood and a fairly unlucky adult life. The reading can be improved if the mountains of the hand are high and rounded: in youth friends and family will give support and love, but adult life will present difficult problems.

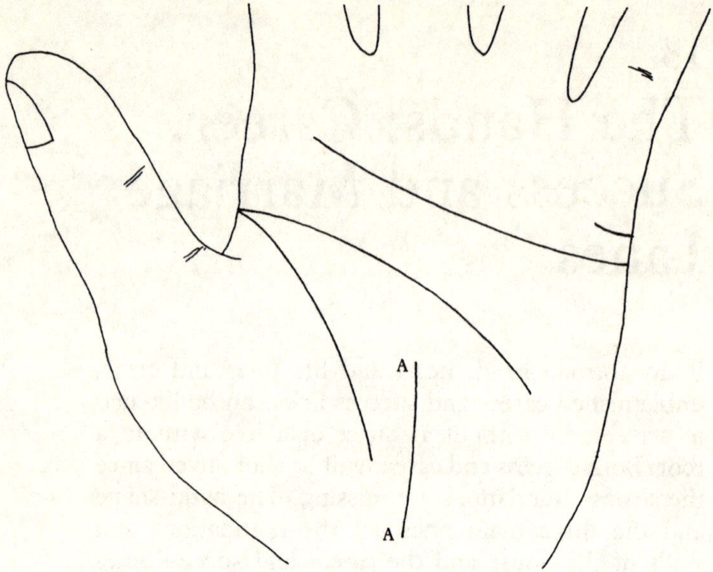

Figure 156

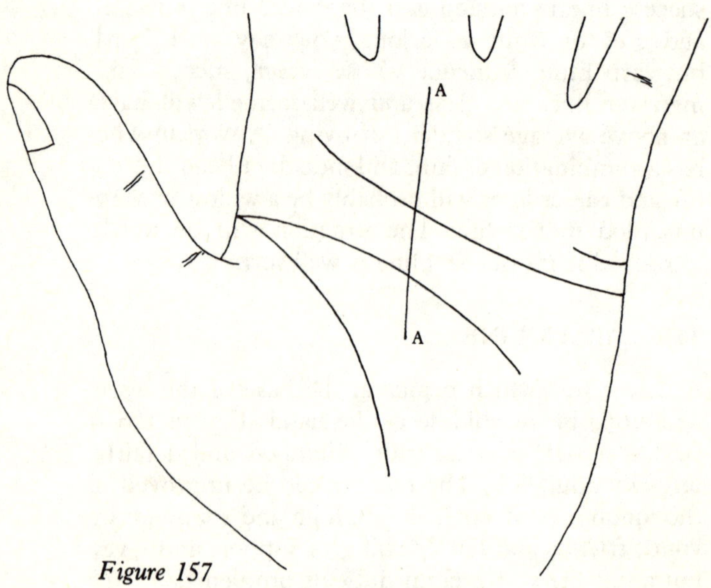

Figure 157

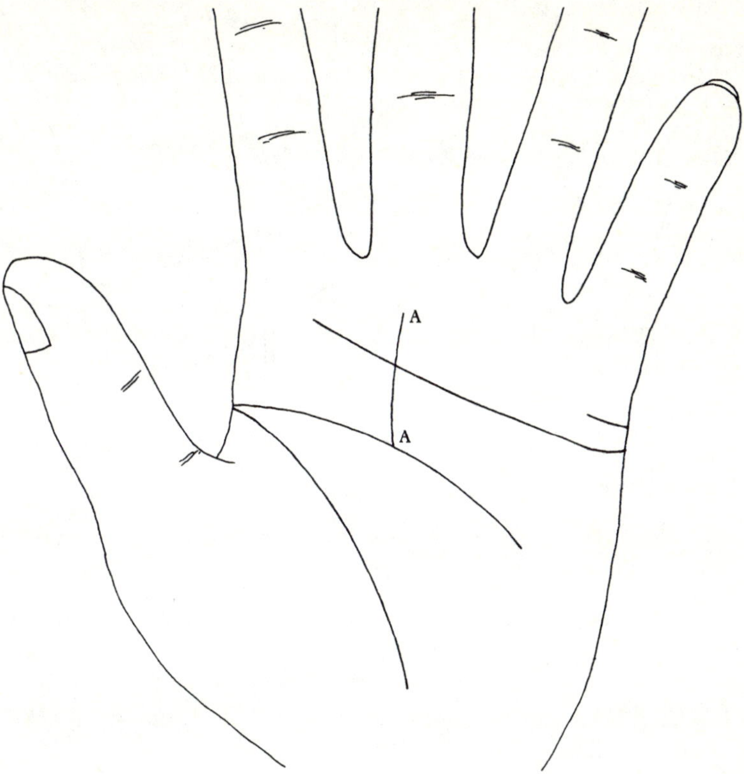

Figure 158

Someone whose career line starts in the middle of the hand and travels up to the middle finger (Figure 157 – AA), and whose hand and three major lines are well formed, will be fortunate in later life. If the career line follows this route but is combined with uneven or irregular mountains, you will struggle until middle age, but from this period onwards your circumstances will improve.

A career line which begins at the head line (Figure 158 – AA) is an indication of opportunities late in life, probably around the age of forty. You will build up a business without financial help from your family.

Sometimes the career line is broken in the middle but there is an additional line running alongside this

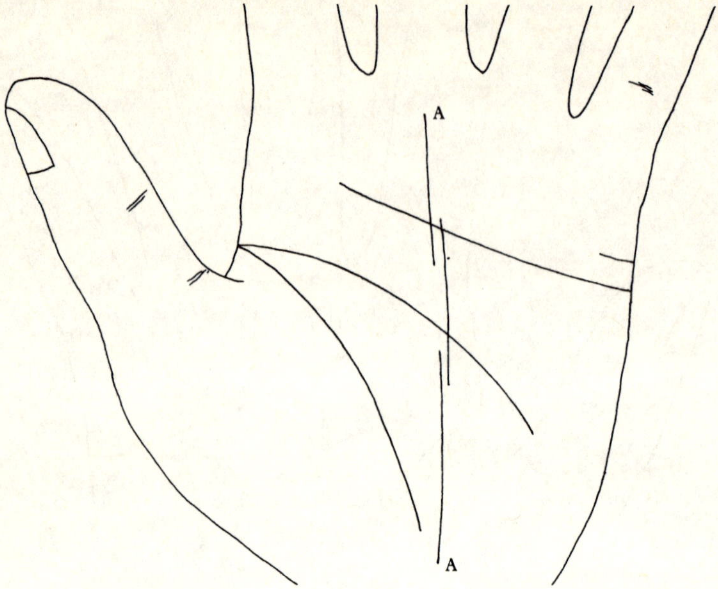

Figure 159

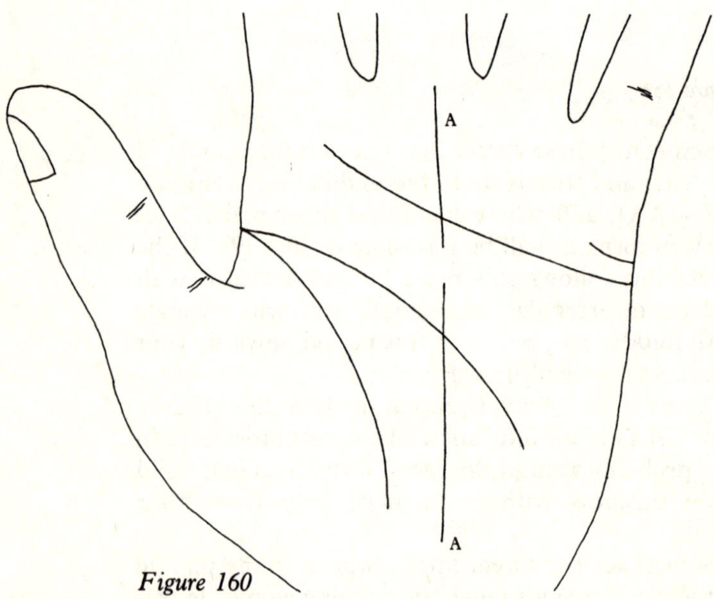

Figure 160

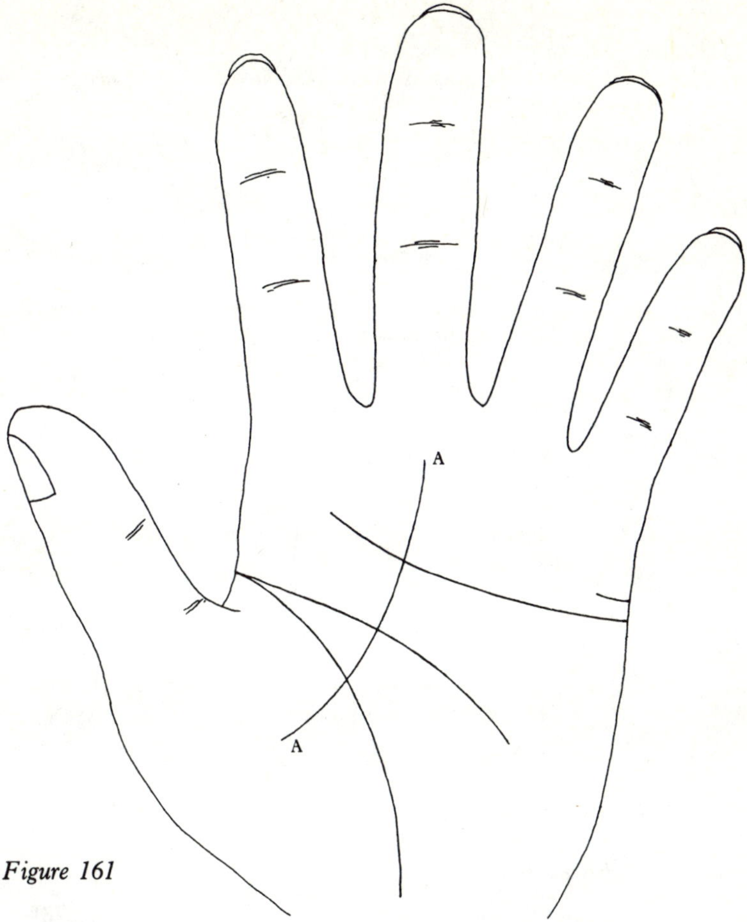

Figure 161

break (Figure 159 – AA). In this case, if the top part of the main line is straighter and clearer than the bottom part, the owner will have an auspicious change of business or career. If the lower part of the line is clearer the change of job will not be so fortunate. A broken career line which lacks a covering line at the side is an indication of unemployment or serious worry (Figure 160 – AA).

The business or career of someone whose line grows from the gold star is flagging due to his over-indulgence (Figure 161 – AA). The Chinese say that such a person 'is drowning in enjoyment'. This reading is particularly applicable if the gold star is very prominent.

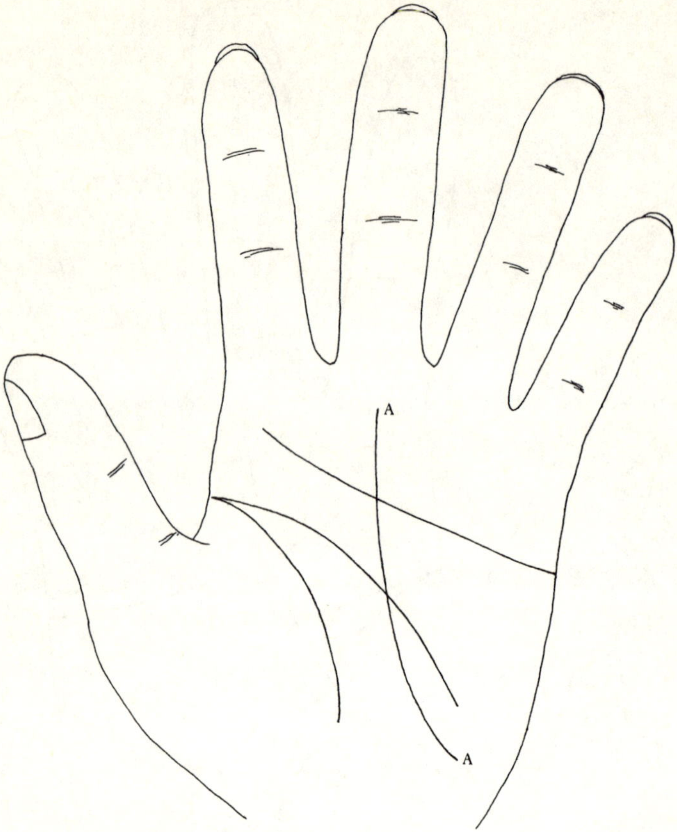

Figure 162

A career line which runs from the moon star is a sign of success in a business partnership (Figure 162 – AA). Someone with this type of career line has no difficulty enlisting the help of others, particularly that of the opposite sex; he is also likely to marry young. This is considered to be a good career line for a woman since she will receive strong support from her husband or partner. If a man has this line in combination with a well-formed hand and straight, unbroken head, heart and life lines, he will be gifted and successful in the arts, either as a composer, actor, writer or artist. This combination can also be seen on the hand of someone adept at speaking on religious matters.

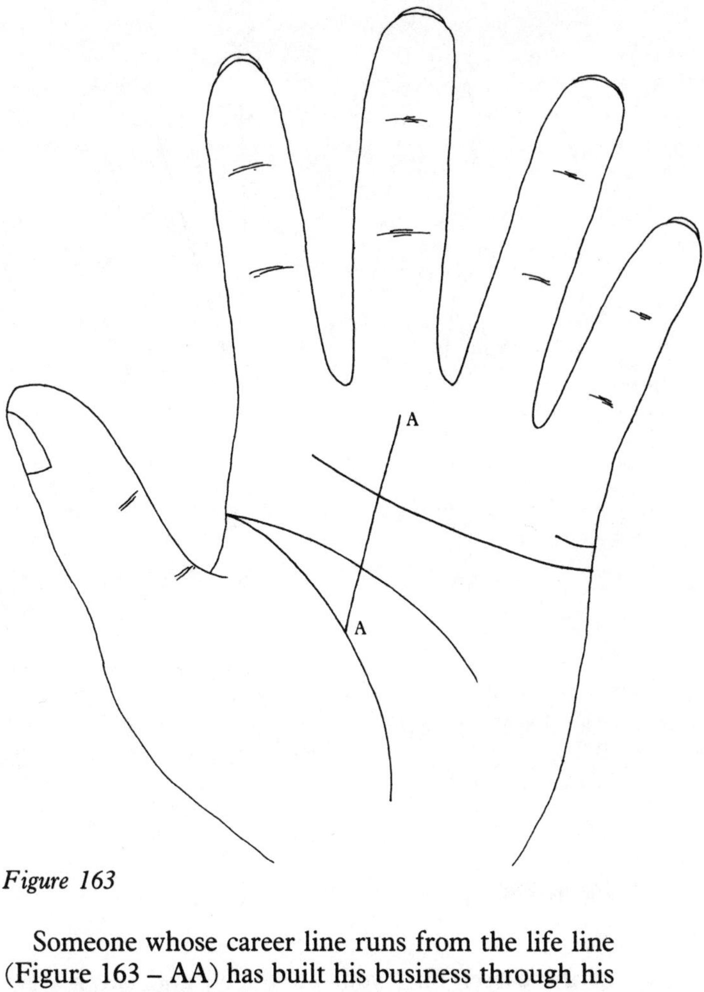

Figure 163

Someone whose career line runs from the life line (Figure 163 – AA) has built his business through his own efforts. But if the career line is broken at many points then business or career is subject to change or unemployment. A career line which grows to a point at the side of the hand between the first finger and thumb is a sign that the owner will lose his business through his hot-tempered nature.

An island at the beginning of the career line signifies difficulties in youth (Figure 164 – a); a man who has this mark on his left hand is not related by blood to his parents – in all likelihood he is adopted. This reading should be taken from a woman's right hand. If both hands have an island at the beginning

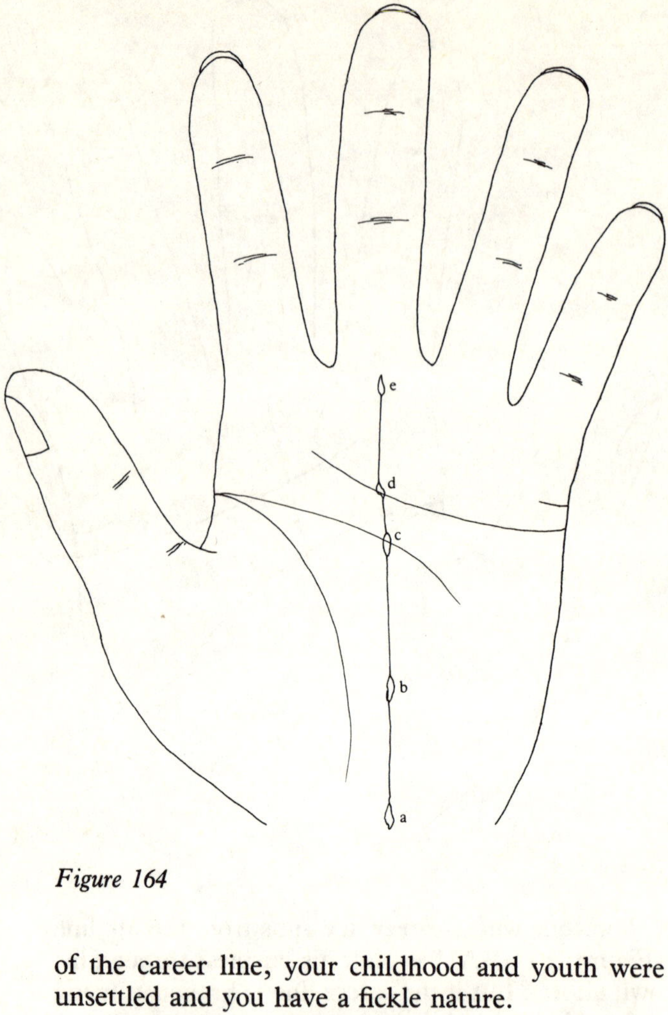

Figure 164

of the career line, your childhood and youth were unsettled and you have a fickle nature.

An island in the middle of the career line signifies business or career trouble (Figure 164 – b), while an island at the point where the head and career lines meet means loss of business through bad planning or bad judgement (Figure 164 – c). An island which is formed at the junction of the career and heart lines denotes loss of a business through an emotional upset involving a spouse or a partner (Figure 164 – d). An island at the end of the career line means loss of a business even though it may have been very successful (Figure 164 – e).

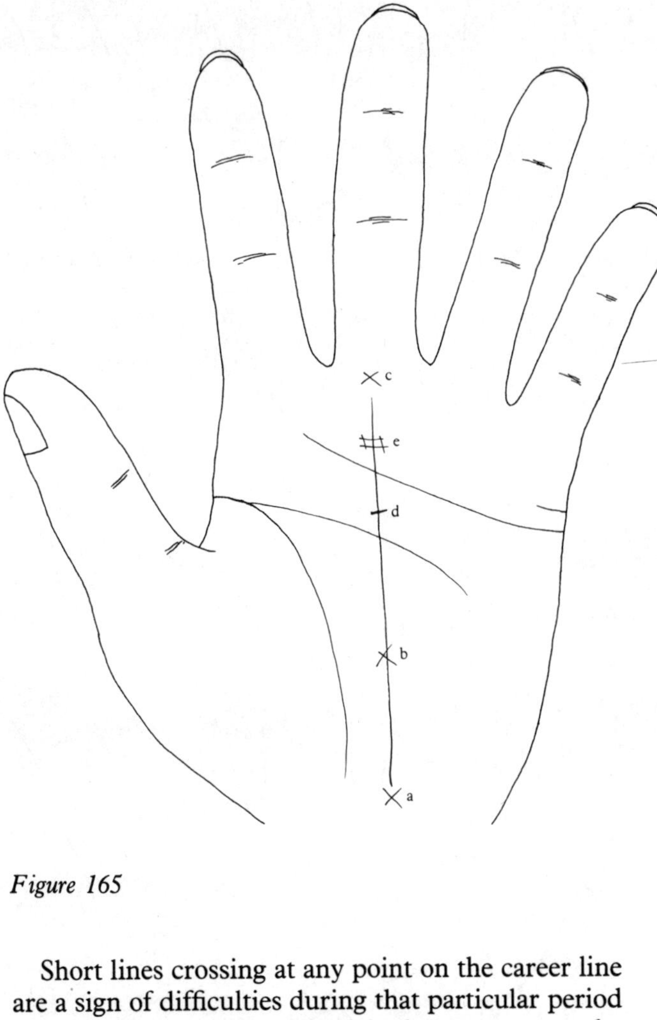

Figure 165

Short lines crossing at any point on the career line are a sign of difficulties during that particular period of life (Figures 165 – a and b) but a cross at the end of the career line signifies death by an accident (Figure 165 – c).

A line which sharply cuts the career line gives an indication of the age at which you will lose a large amount of money or even your business (Figure 165 – d). If the lines which cross the career line form a square, a friend will arrive with much needed help when severe problems crop up. This is known by the Chinese as a 'noble square' (Figure 165 – e).

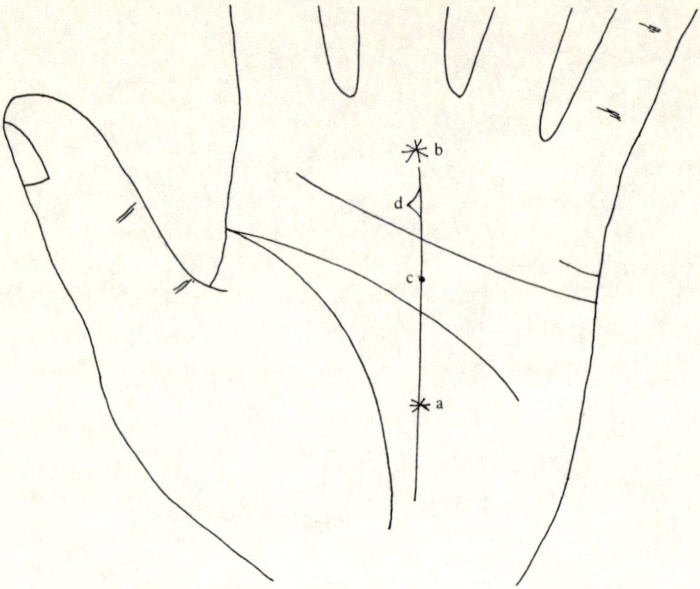

Figure 166

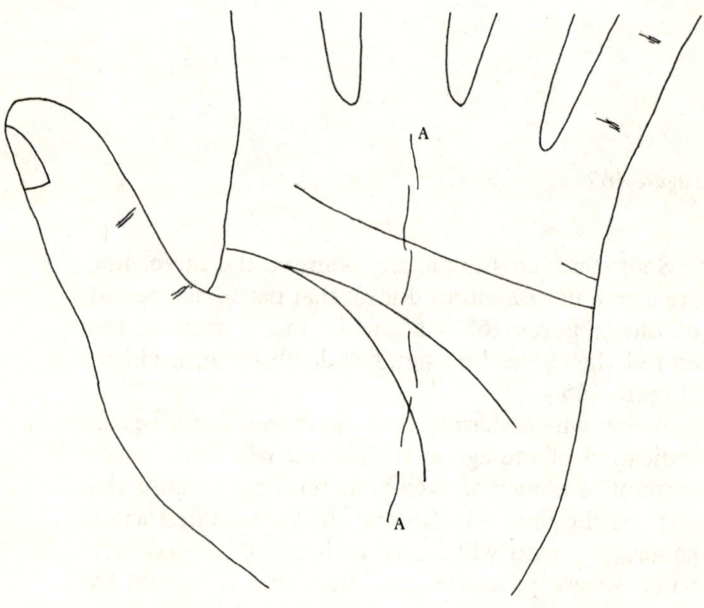

Figure 167

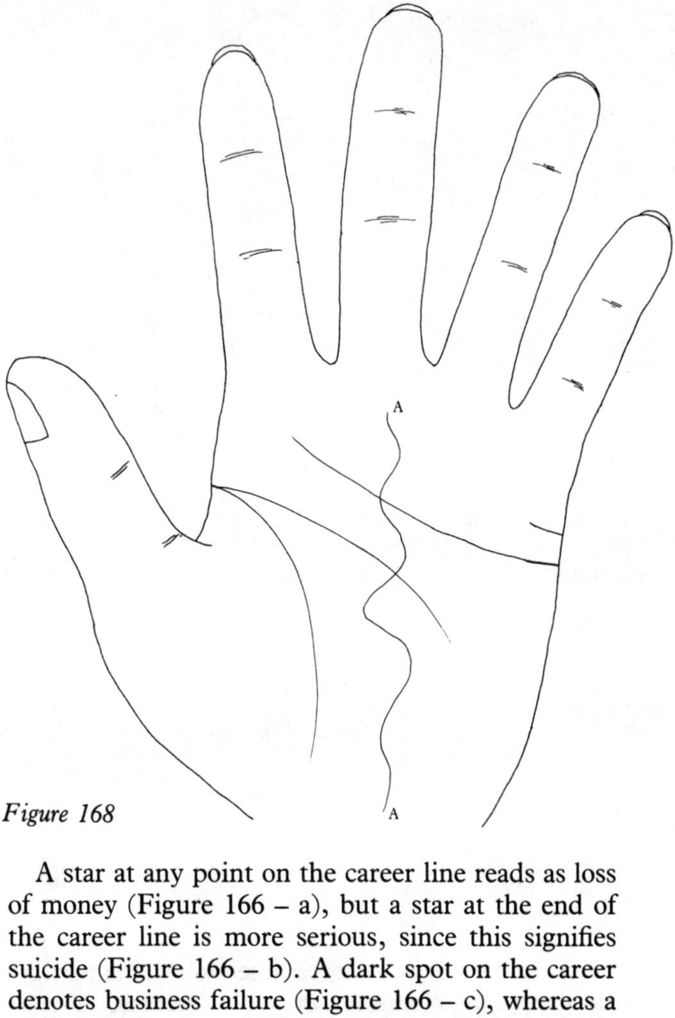

Figure 168

A star at any point on the career line reads as loss of money (Figure 166 – a), but a star at the end of the career line is more serious, since this signifies suicide (Figure 166 – b). A dark spot on the career denotes business failure (Figure 166 – c), whereas a triangle means considerable improvements in business or career (Figure 166 – d). A broken career line is a sign that your business will fail many times (Figure 167 – AA). Frequent job changes and dissatisfaction with work can be predicted from a wavy career line (Figure 168 – AA).

THE SUCCESS LINE

The success line supports the business line and is in indication of your disposition. If you have a distinct

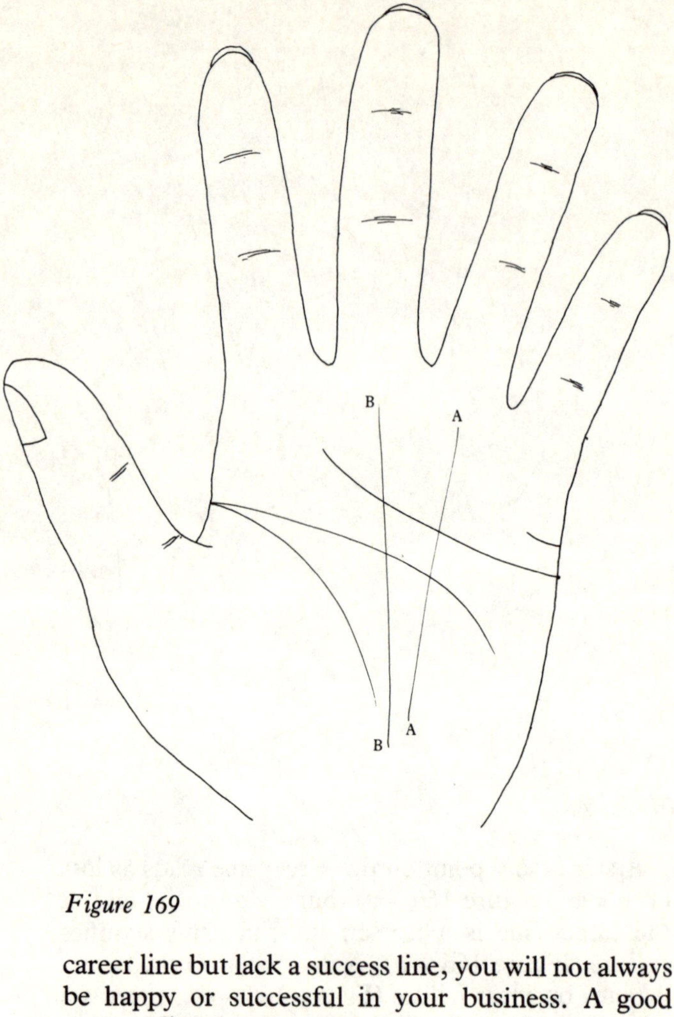

Figure 169

career line but lack a success line, you will not always be happy or successful in your business. A good success line but no career line is a sign of easily acquired wealth; however, it is likely to come from a dishonest or immoral source. The Chinese fortune-tellers say that a woman with a success line but no career line is not respected by other people. Both the career and success line have important positions on the hand so it is better not to have these lines than to have ones that are badly broken or badly formed.

The ideal success line is straight, deep and thin, and stretches from the base of the hand up to the

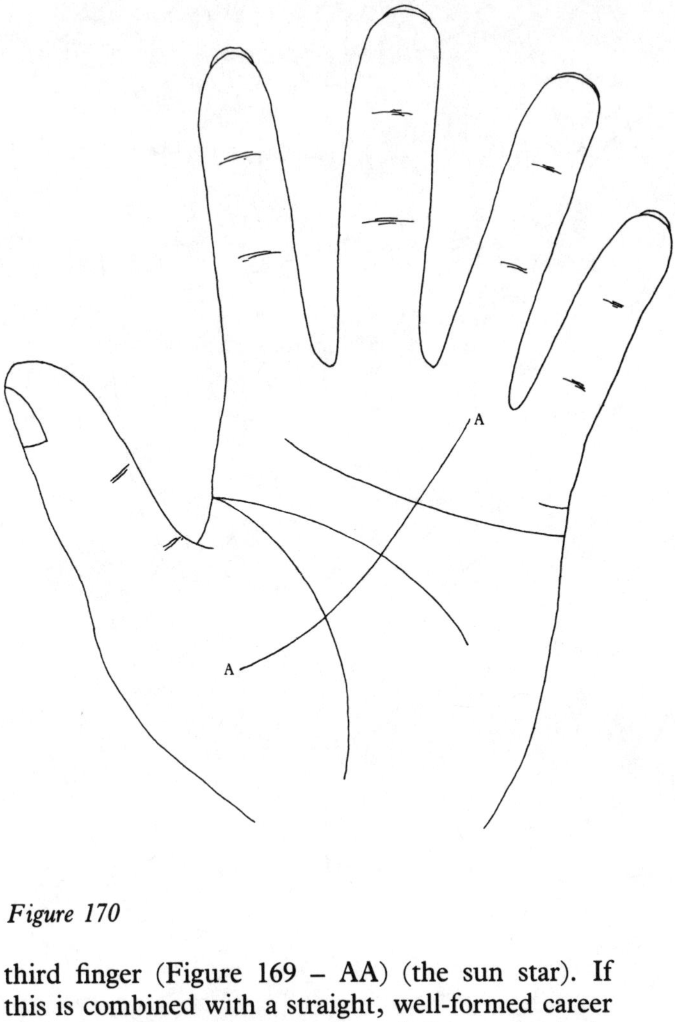

Figure 170

third finger (Figure 169 – AA) (the sun star). If this is combined with a straight, well-formed career line you will be guaranteed good fortune early in life, your progress will be smooth and lucky and you will never be troubled by financial worries (Figure 169 – BB. A success line which reaches from the gold star to the sun star is the sign of a happy and wealthy family background; you will also have a good marriage and a successful career (Figure 170 – AA).

A success line which travels from the moon star up to the sun star denotes success only in a partnership formed with one or more people. It is also the sign

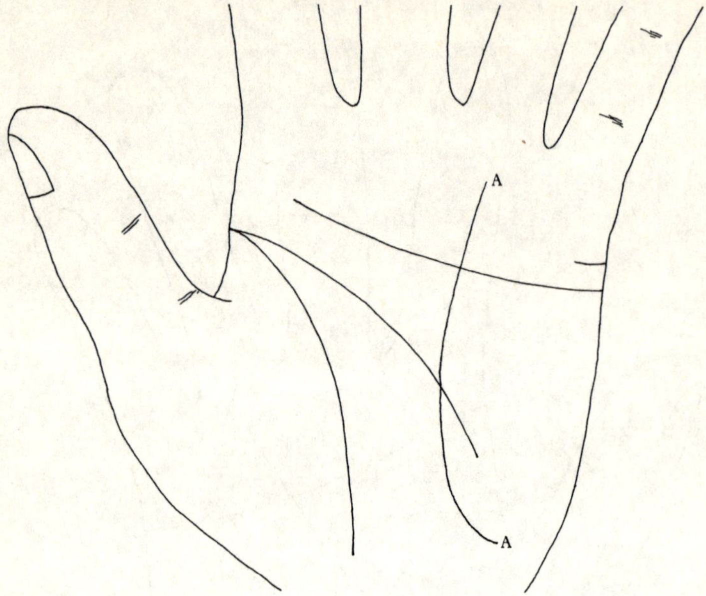

Figure 171

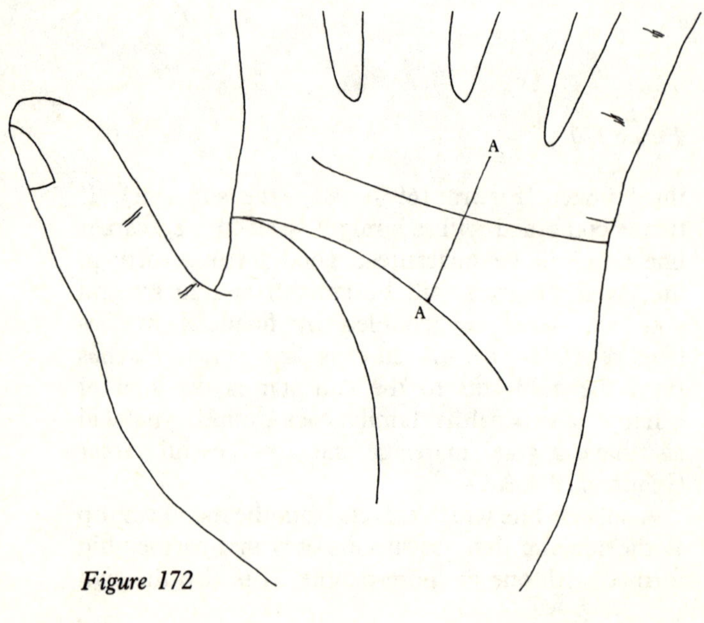

Figure 172

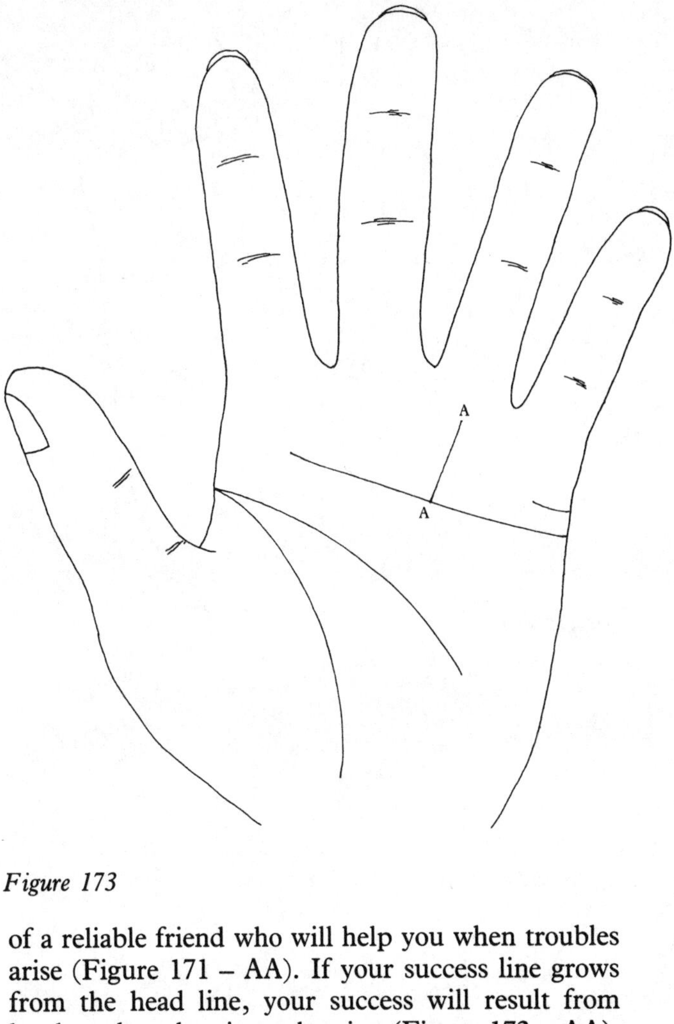

Figure 173

of a reliable friend who will help you when troubles arise (Figure 171 – AA). If your success line grows from the head line, your success will result from hard work and serious planning (Figure 172 – AA). Once again, this success line must be combined with a good career line. A success line which stems from the heart line denotes business success after fifty years of age; if this line is particularly clear and straight then you will be famous in the arts both during your life and after your death (Figure 173 – AA).

Someone whose success line leads straight from the life line to the sun star will be successful in business, and although he will have many initial

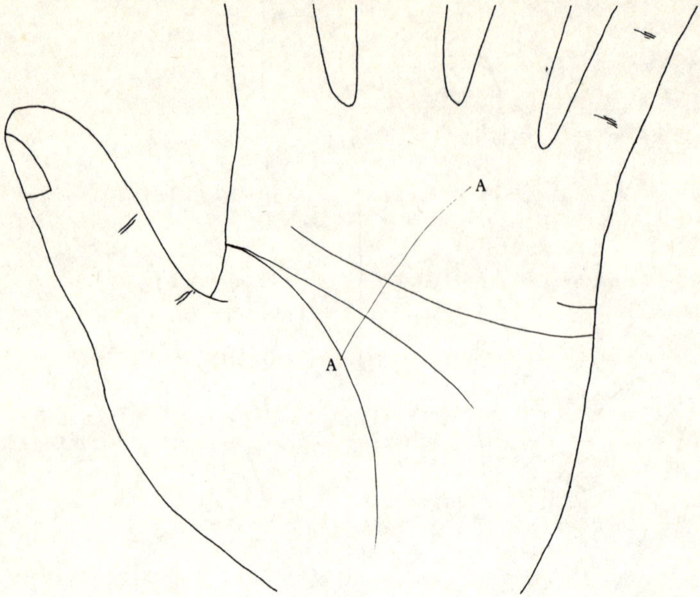

Figure 174

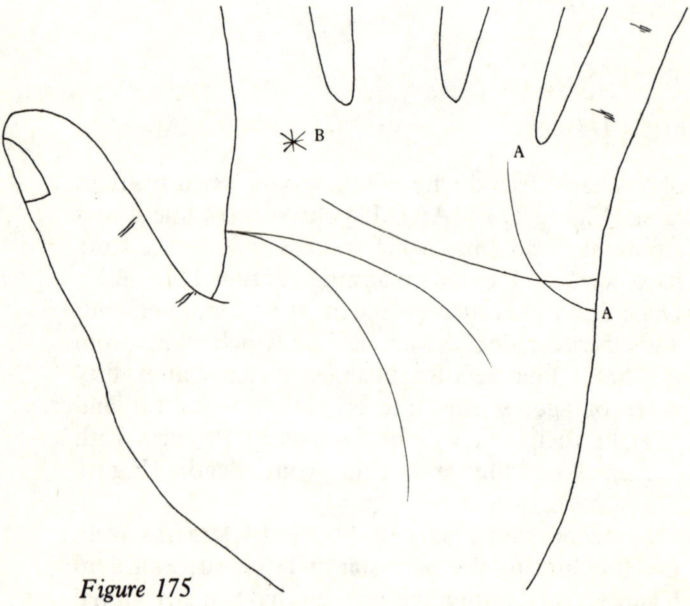

Figure 175

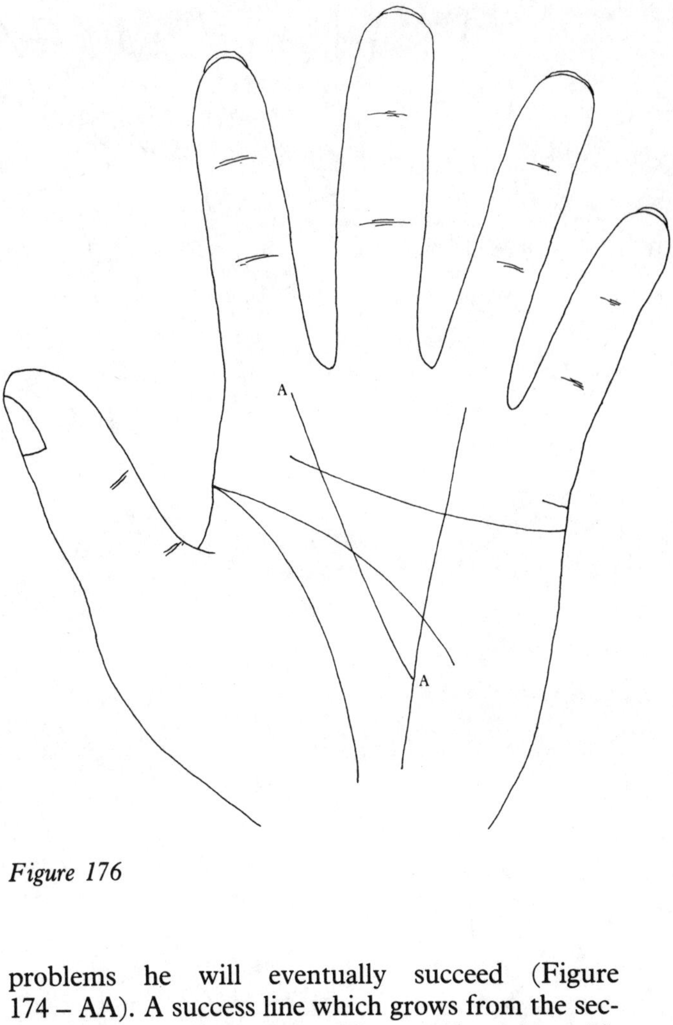

Figure 176

problems he will eventually succeed (Figure 174 – AA). A success line which grows from the second fire star to the sun star (Figure 175 – AA) and is combined with a straight career line is a sign of a disciplined nature; you are suited to the armed forces, for example. If you also have lines forming a star in the wood star, you will attain a high rank in the army or in a disciplined organization (Figure 175 – B). An additional line which forks from the success line up to the wood star is an indication that you will be offered a high-ranking position in the job which you least expected to receive (Figure 176 – AA).

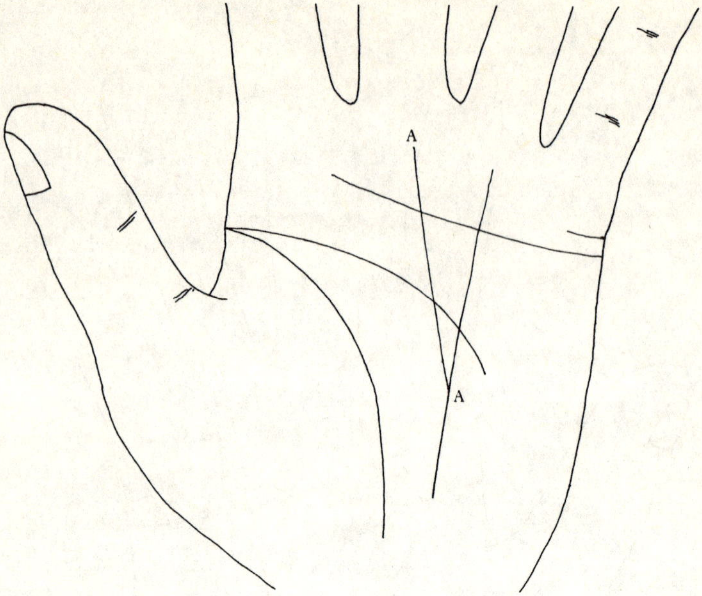

Figure 177

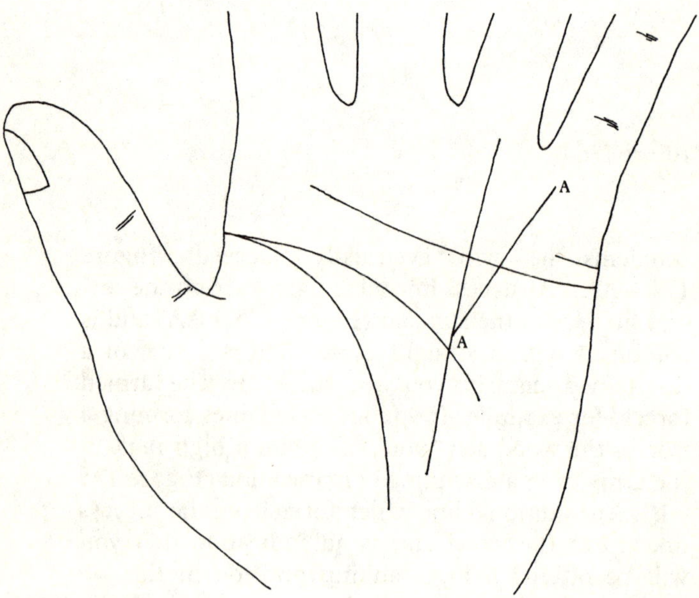

Figure 178

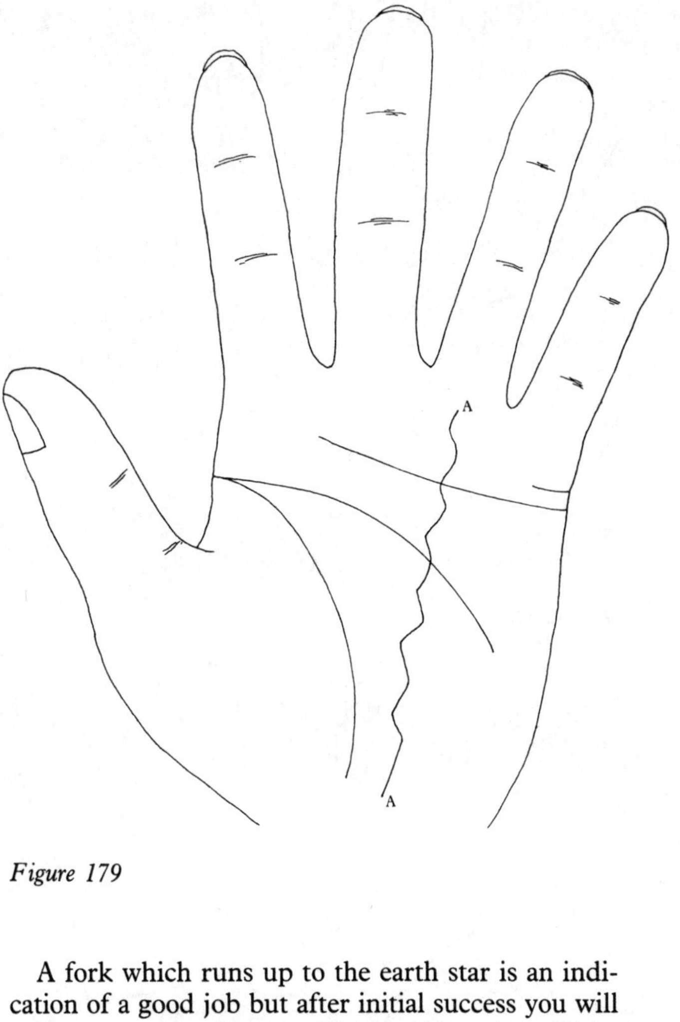

Figure 179

A fork which runs up to the earth star is an indication of a good job but after initial success you will suffer a considerable loss (Figure 177 – AA). If the line forks towards the water star, you will be gifted in commerce or science and will be famous during your life (Figure 178 – AA). A wavy success line denotes hard work but little success, and a grey or white success line will give the same reading (Figure 179 – AA). A success line which stops in the middle of the hand is a sign of success in the early years of your career, but by middle age you will lose everything. You will never have an opportunity to make good your loss (Figure 180 – AA). If the success line

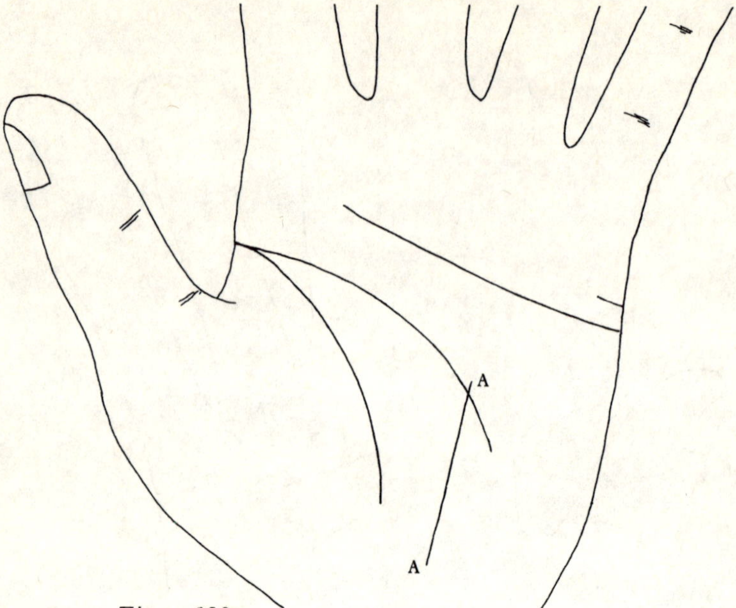

Figure 180

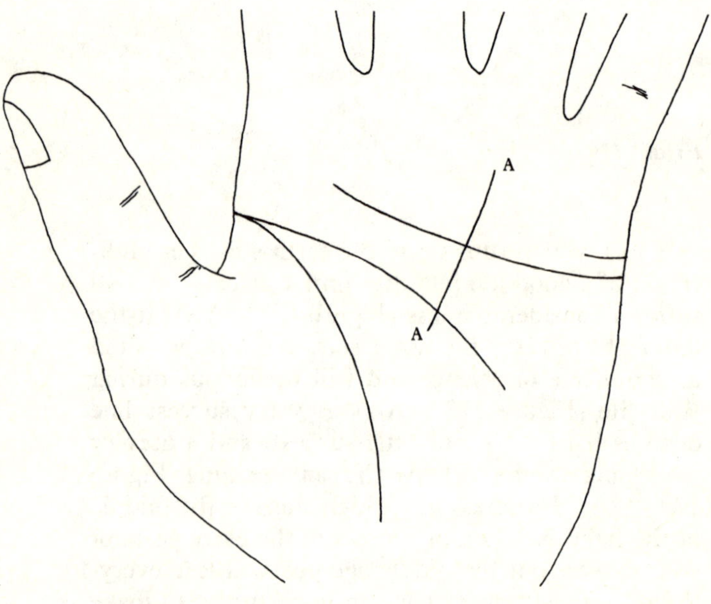

Figure 181

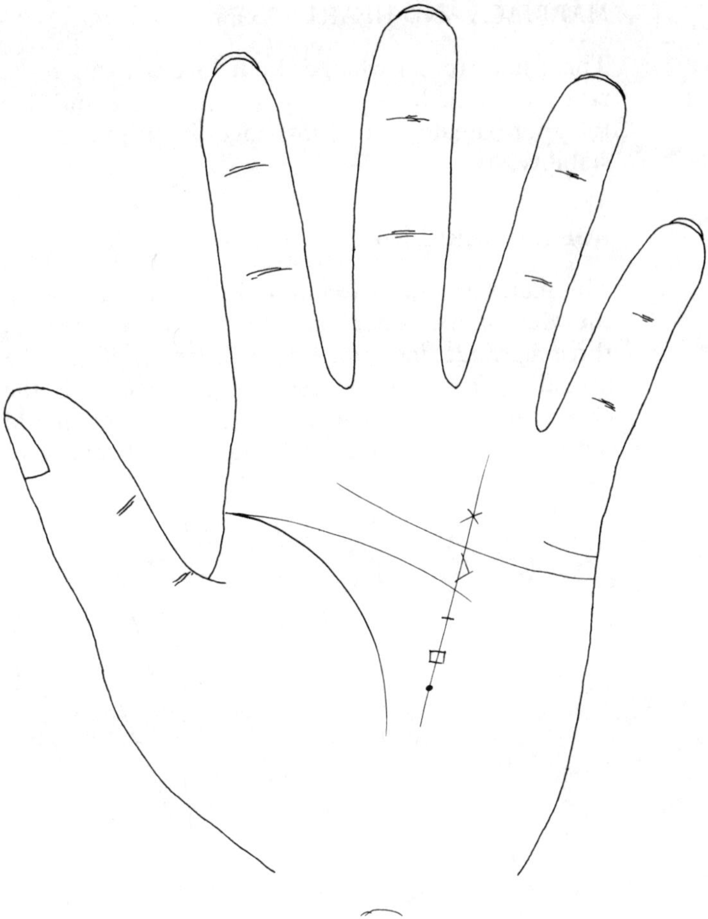

Figure 182

reaches from the middle of the hand to the sun star, you will be poor before middle age but successful afterwards (Figure 181 – AA). A success line cut by a straight line, two cross-shaped lines or a black spot is a sign of current misfortune (Figure 182).

A triangle or a square on the success line is a helpful sign which will sort out any difficulties. A star on the success line is auspicious whereas a star on the career line is unlucky. If you have more than one success line, this does not mean that you will be twice or three times as lucky; the reading should be taken from one success line only.

MARRIAGE AND HEART LINES

These lines reveal whether your love is likely to be false, true, lucky or unlucky. They also indicate the approximate year of marriage, its length and its stability.

AGE AT MARRIAGE

The marriage line is found above the heart line, in the area of the water star. You may have two or three marriage lines which vary in length; if so, take a reading from the longest, straightest line. If the chosen line is closest to the heart line, you should marry between the ages of eighteen and twenty-two

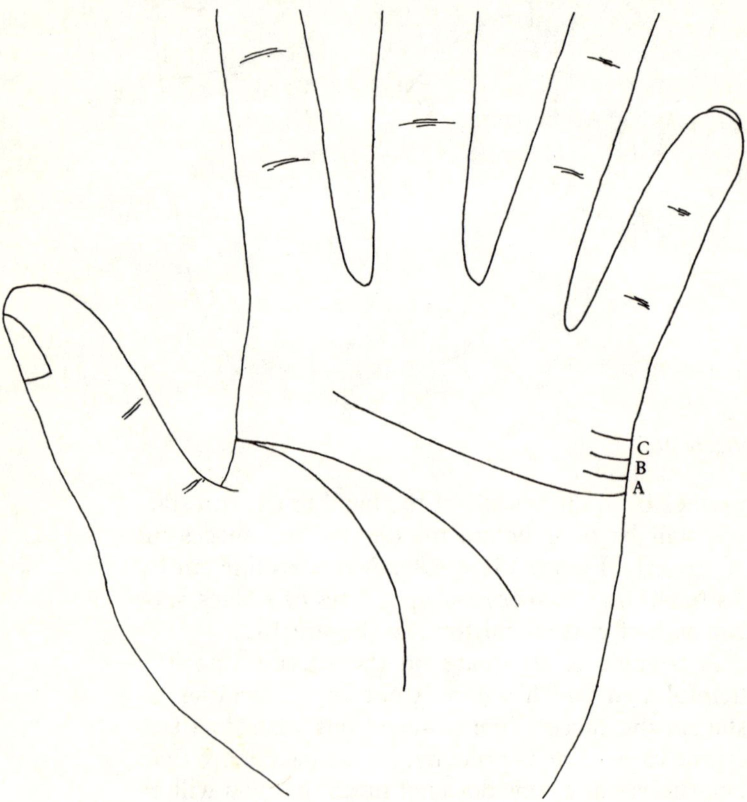

Figure 183

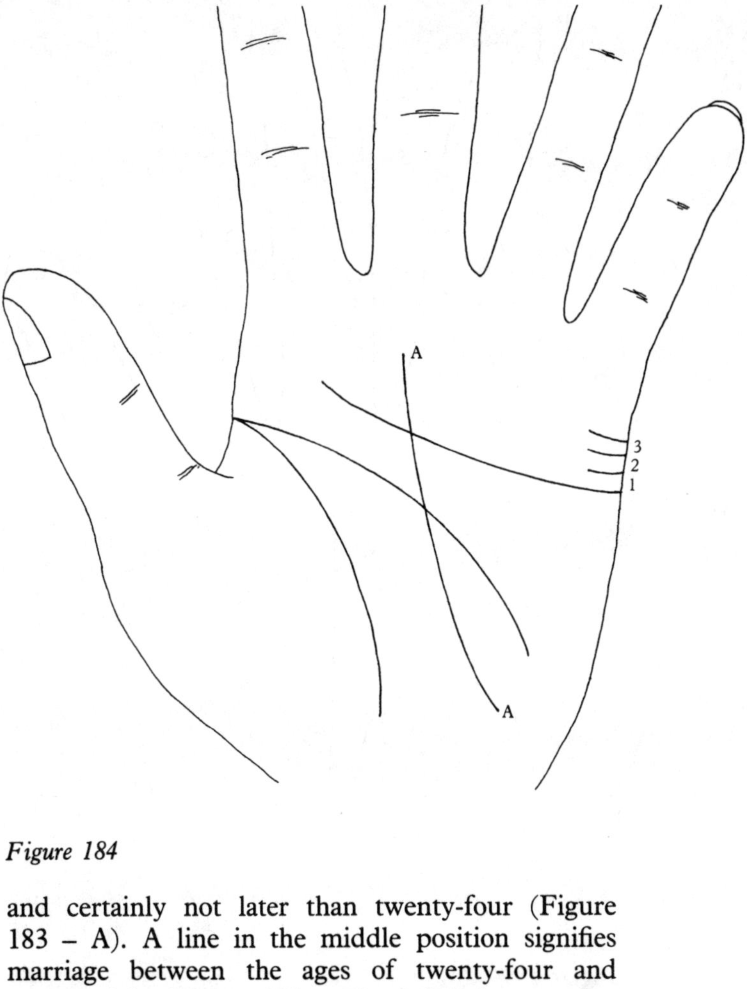

Figure 184

and certainly not later than twenty-four (Figure 183 – A). A line in the middle position signifies marriage between the ages of twenty-four and twenty-eight (Figure 183 – B); definitely not after the age of thirty-two. The last line, which is nearest to the base of the little finger, represents marriage from thirty-two years and above (Figure 183 – C). If you do not marry during the year range indicated by the straightest marriage line, wait until later in life; if you also have crooked or broken lines, again it is advisable to wait and marry later in life. If you want to marry before the age indicated by your marriage line, you must check that the gold star is well rounded and the career line reaches from the moon star to the earth star (Figure 184 – AA).

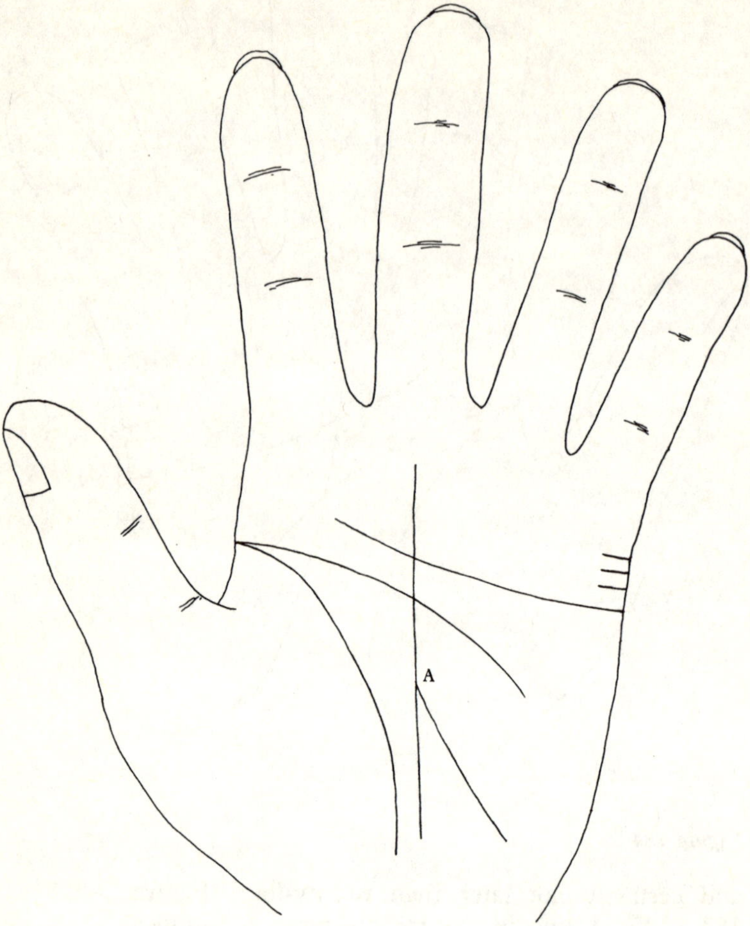

Figure 185

The marriage line does not always control the time of your marriage. The marriage age can also be calculated if you have a line running from the moon star to the career line. The marrying age is estimated from the point at which the two lines meet (Figure 185 – A). Two lines crossing in the wood star also help to determine someone's age at marriage. If the crossing lines are close to the head line, marriage will occur quite early in life (Figure 186 – a), but if the crossed lines on the wood star are far from the head line then it is advisable to wait until the early

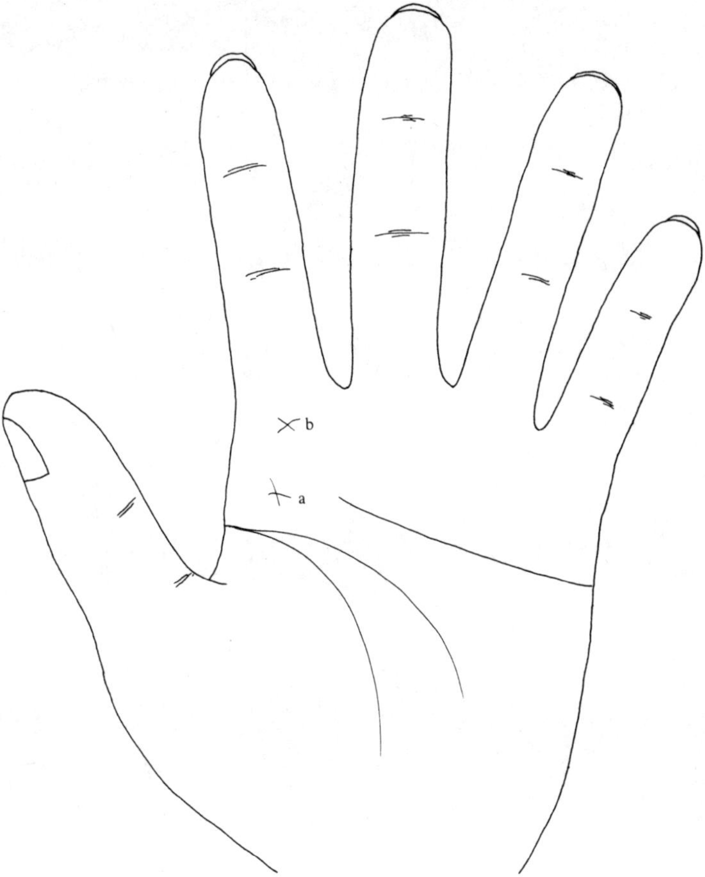

Figure 186

thirties before marrying (Figure 186 – b). The Chinese say that this cross has the strength to override the reading given on the marriage line.

THE MARRIAGE LINE

Someone whose marriage line slopes down towards the head line wants affairs outside marriage. Because of his flirtatious nature misunderstandings often develop with other people. Although he has no intention of harming others, he succeeds in doing so since

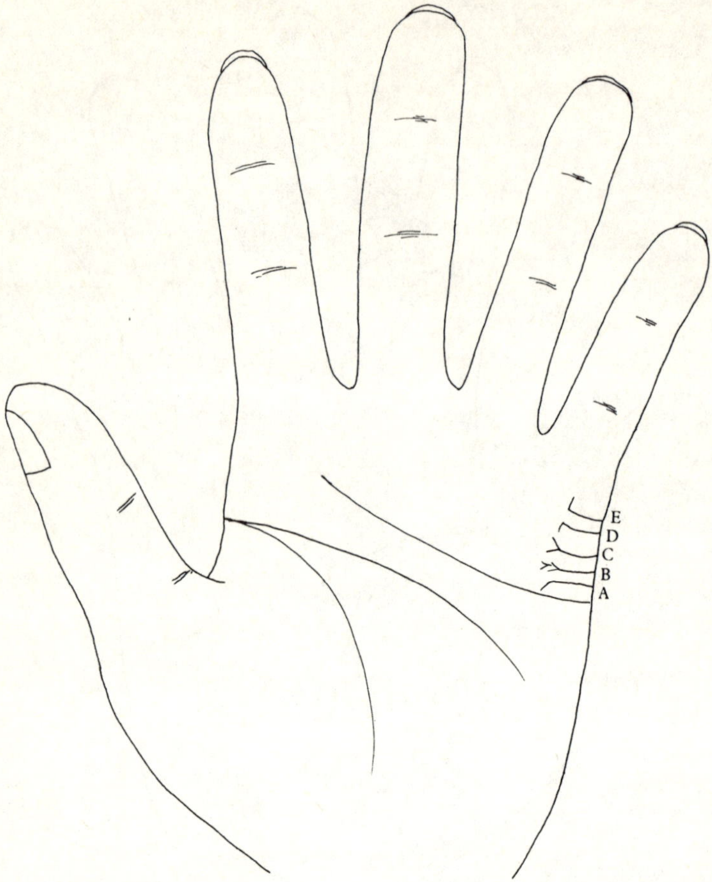

Figure 187

he is fickle. A marriage line which slopes down towards the heart line so that they almost touch is a sign of separation (Figure 187 – A). If this line crosses the heart line, it is an indication of a divorce. A marriage line which branches out at the end like a small palm tree denotes marriage difficulties which will eventually be resolved (Figure 187 – B). A marriage line which has two diverging lines at the end means that the marriage will be quite successful but one partner will die sooner than expected or there will be a divorce (Figure 187 – C).

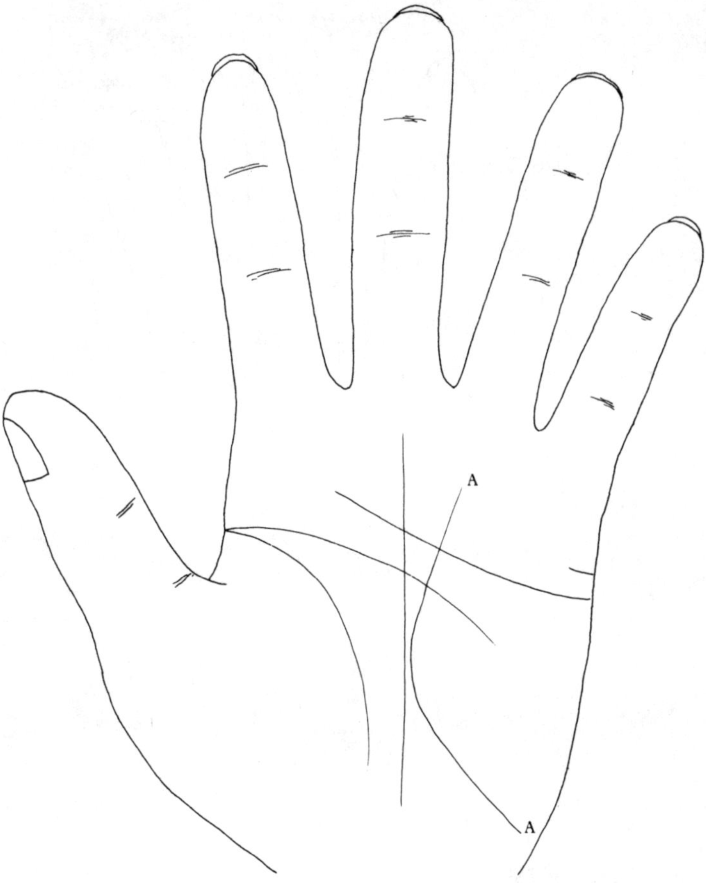

Figure 188

The wife of a man whose marriage line bends down to form a hook will die by accident (Figure 187 – D). If the hook grows upwards, the marriage will be unsuccessful since he will always regret the chance of lost love (Figure 187 – E). If the career line is met at an angle by a line from the moon star and the success line rises from this angle, then the marriage will be happy and the husband and wife will be extremely wealthy (Figure 188 – AA). If this line from the moon star passes straight through the career line, the marriage will not be successful

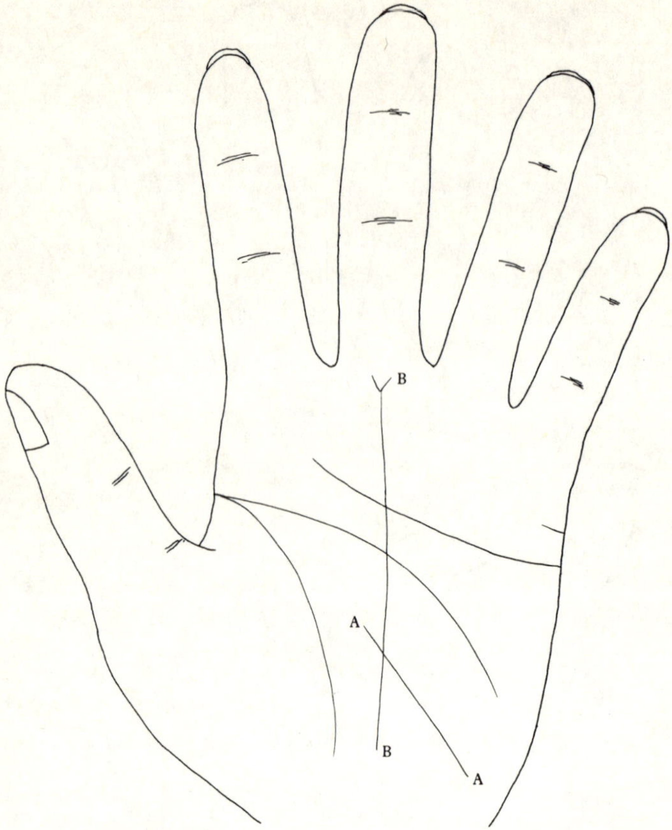

Figure 189

(Figure 189 – AA). However, a career line which forks at its tip is a sign that the couple will eventually find happiness together (Figure 189 – BB).

A wavy marriage line denotes an unsuccessful marriage, since you are aiming at an ideal married life which can never be attained (Figure 190 – A). As the Chinese say, 'You see a flower in the mirror, you see the moon in the water.' A man whose marriage line forks at the edge of the hand will be unfaithful to his future wife before marriage (Figure 190 – B). If the fork occurs on a woman's hand, her husband will probably leave her soon after they are married. Unmarried women who have this sign are likely to be cheated by men.

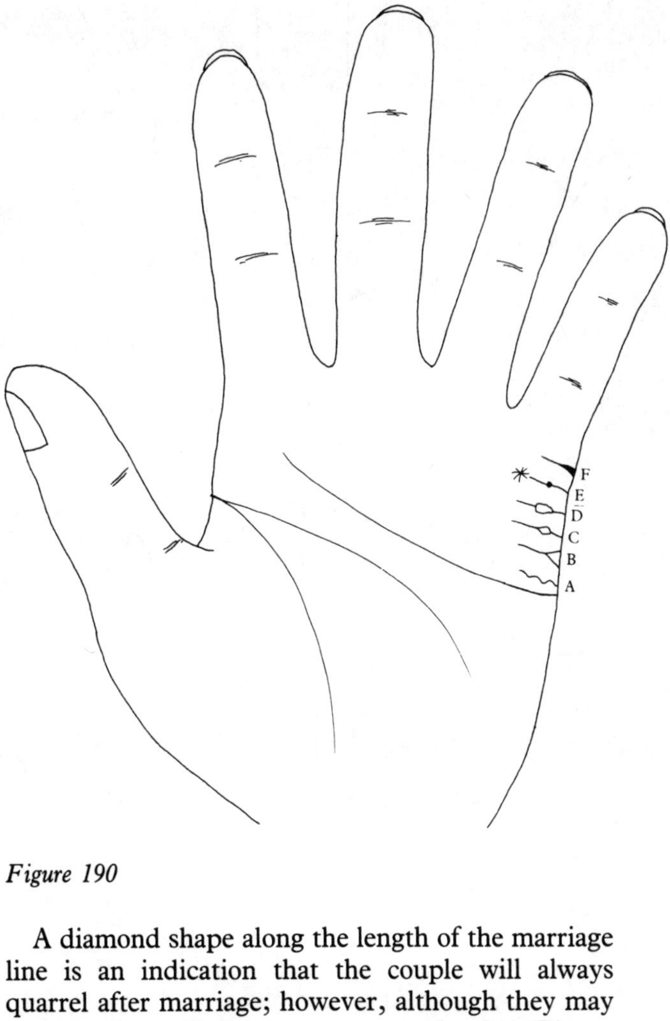

Figure 190

A diamond shape along the length of the marriage line is an indication that the couple will always quarrel after marriage; however, although they may separate they will always return to each other (Figure 190 – C). An island on the marriage line means divorce or separation (Figure 190 – D), while a dark spot or a star at the end is an indication of the sudden death of a partner (Figure 190 – E). Someone whose marriage line is thick at the beginning and then narrows will be passionate at the start of his relationship, then his ardour will cool (Figure 190 – F). However, he will not get divorced.

A line which runs from the moon star to the career line is known as the effective line; it can affect the

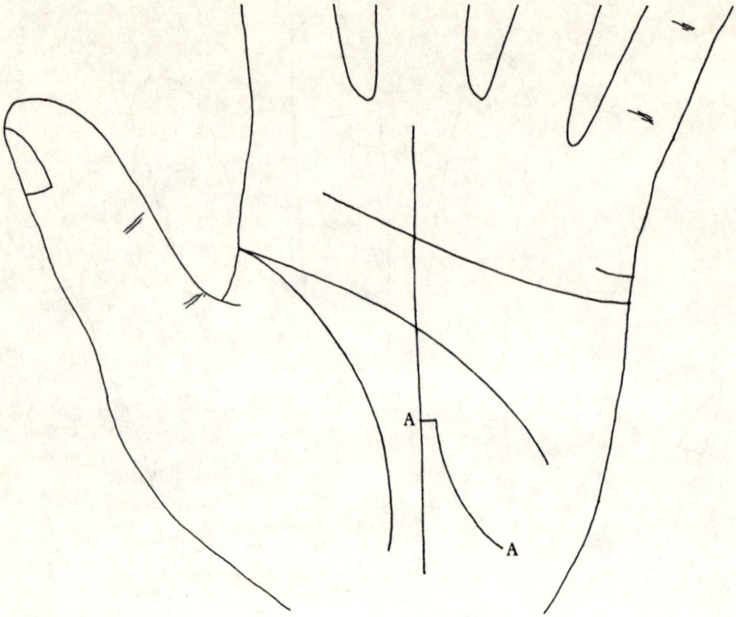

Figure 191

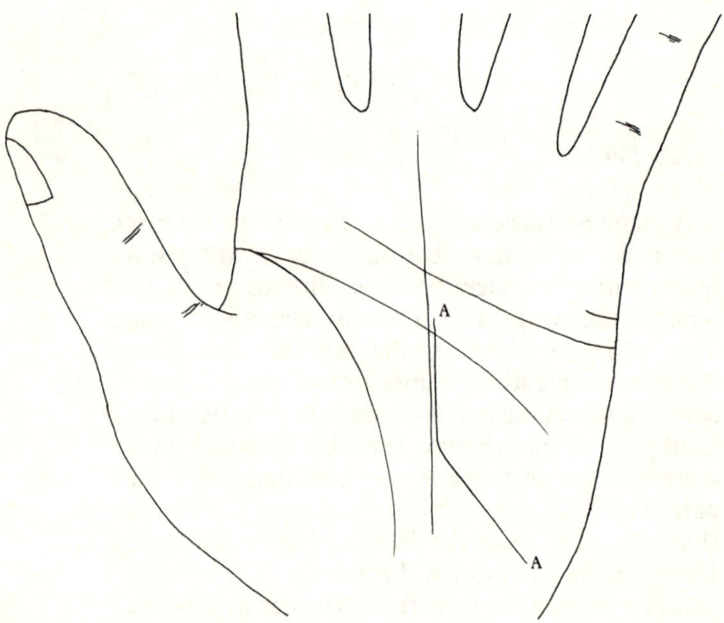

Figure 192

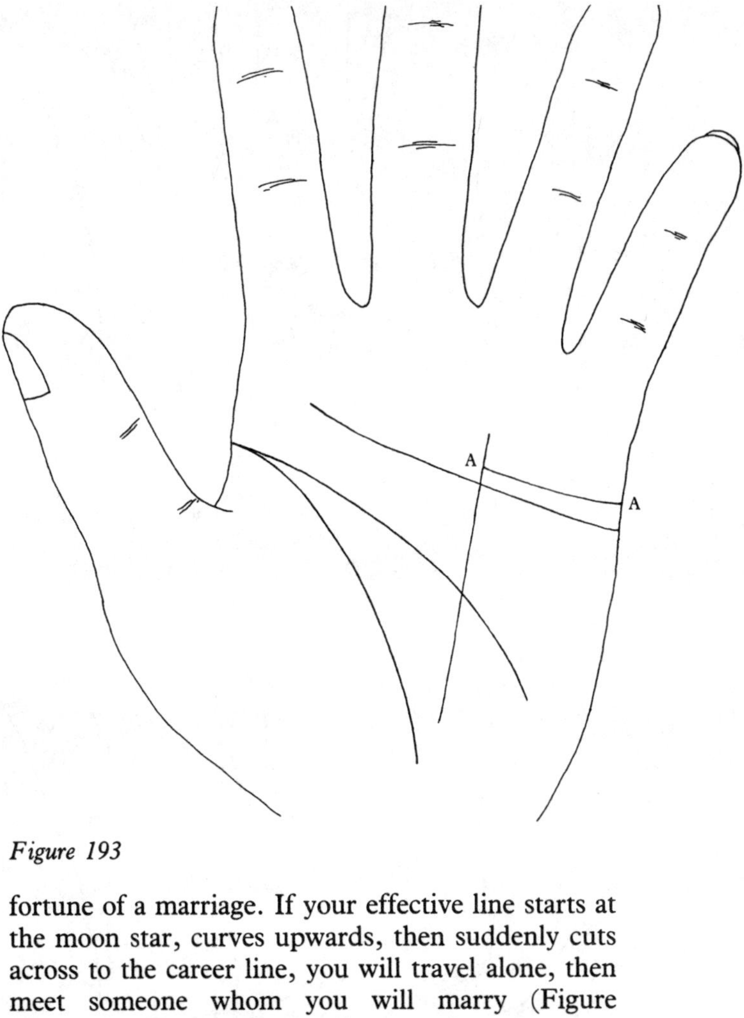

Figure 193

fortune of a marriage. If your effective line starts at the moon star, curves upwards, then suddenly cuts across to the career line, you will travel alone, then meet someone whom you will marry (Figure 191 – AA). If your effective line runs from the moon star up to the career line and then runs parallel to the career line, you will love someone dearly but will never be able to marry (Figure 192 – AA).

Someone who has two marriage lines which are both straight and long will have a lover before marriage and will continue the affair even after marriage. A marriage line which touches the success line is an indication of marriage to a wealthy person (Figure 193 – AA). If a small line touches the marriage line and then runs parallel to the success line,

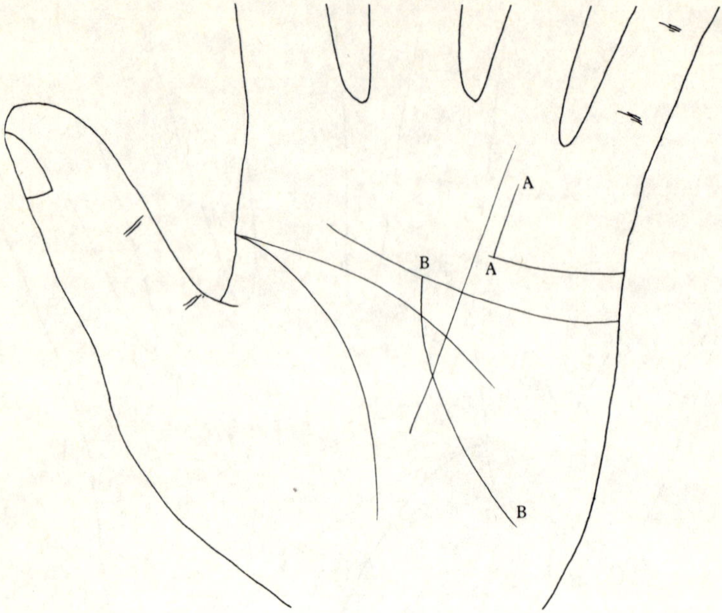

Figure 194

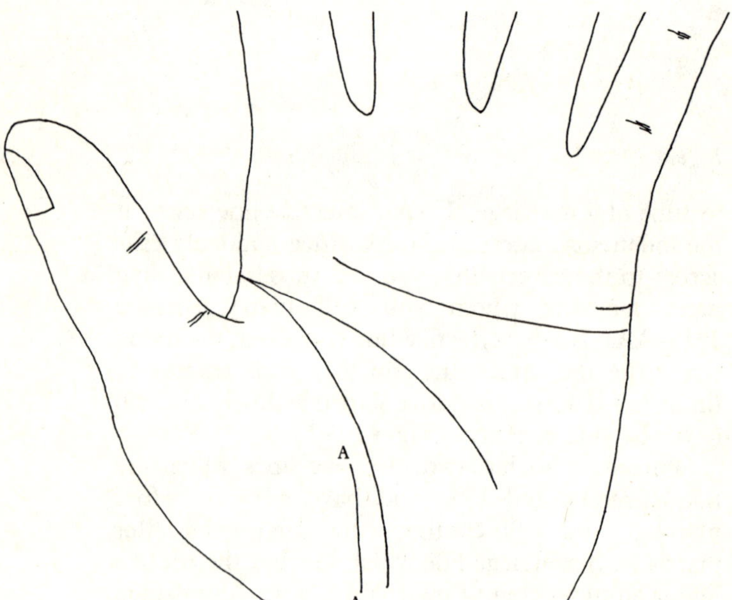

Figure 195

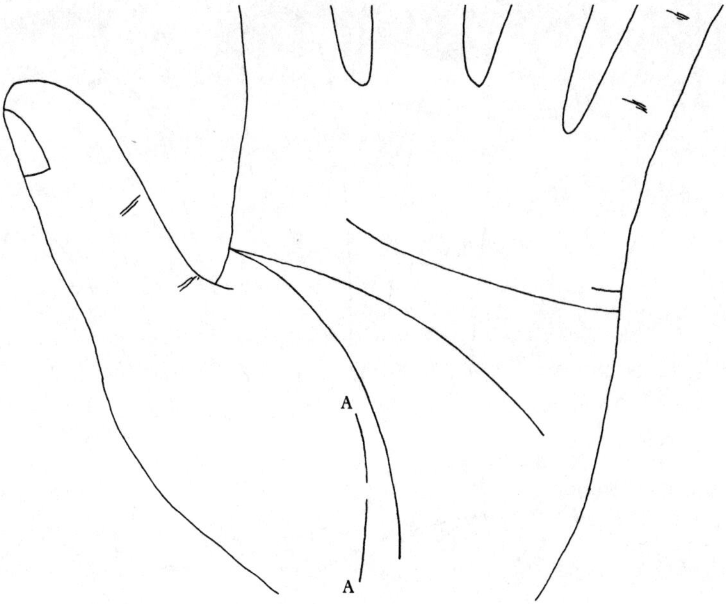

Figure 196

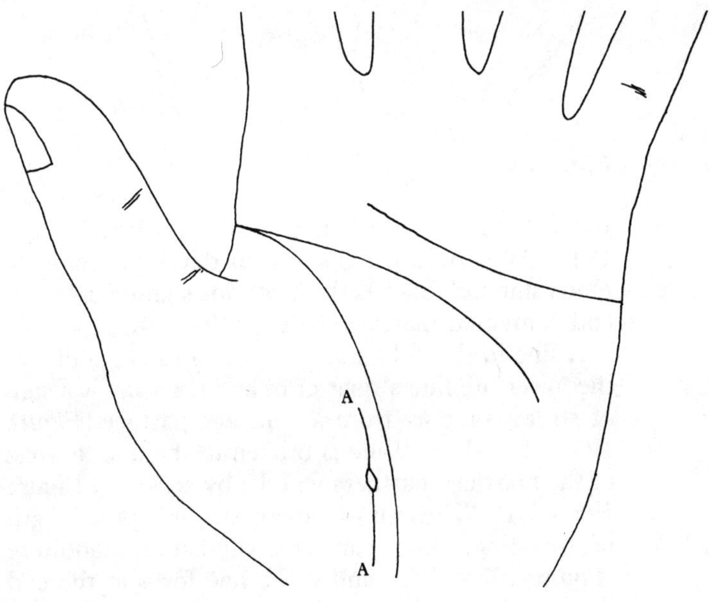

Figure 197

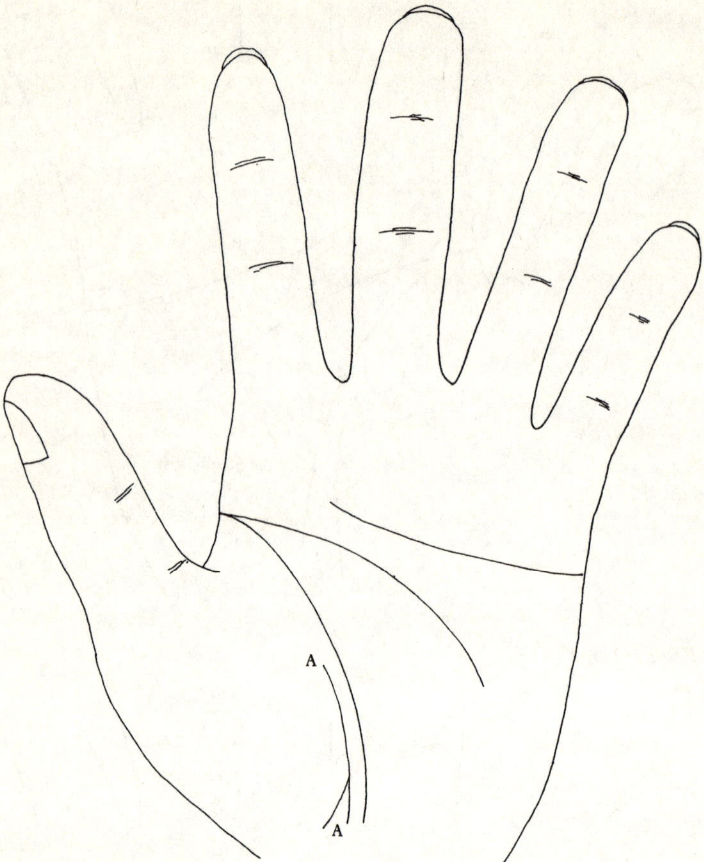

Figure 198

you will be rich and famous after marriage (Figure 194 – AA). A career line which develops from the moon star and touches the heart line signifies a happy and contented marriage (Figure 194 – BB).

A line in the gold star area which runs parallel to the lower life line a quarter of an inch away is a sign of strong support from a marriage partner (Figure 195 – AA). If this line is broken in the middle, one of the marriage partners will die by accident (Figure 196 – AA). When an island appears along the length of this line, both partners will commit adultery (Figure 197 – AA), and if the line forks at the end there will be a divorce or separation (Figure 198 – AA).

14 Epilogue

In this book we have been able to give you some of the teachings of the ancient Chinese art of physiognomy. Drawing upon the traditional books which are still to be found at the elbow of every present-day diviner, we have opened a door onto this barely explored world. *Lines of Destiny* offers a part, albeit the most popular part, of the corpus of physiognomical teachings. The *Ma-i*, *Pa P'u Tzu* and the *Golden Scissors* are simply the most accessible and readily interpretable of the many tomes which make up the library of traditional wisdom on this subject.

In the past it has been all too common for Westerners to dismiss such books, practitioners and beliefs as nothing but superstition. Equally the reverse has been true, namely overcredulous Westerners have sought to swallow totally the practices of physiognomy while failing to give real thought or credence to the profound beliefs which actually underpin them. Neither of these approaches is particularly helpful or honest and both have led to Chinese practitioners feeling very cautious about sharing their teachings with non-Chinese. Our hope in producing this book is that we have managed to strike a balance between these two extremes.

As we have shown, Chinese physiognomy is not just a random set of speculations, but is a very particular and at times illustrative way into traditional Chinese beliefs of life and death, fate and destiny, good and evil, Heaven and Earth and the very nature of humanity. However, we have also shown that a very healthy Chinese strain of doubt has always been present which has helped to temper the teachings of the physiognomists and to keep alive a debate about those more profound areas of religious speculation such as rebirth and fate. Either one without the other would be a misbalance.

In the team which worked on this book there were some Chinese and Westerners who were willing to accept the validity of the teachings and others who were not. What united us was a belief that, whether it is 'true' or not, this was and is an important dimension of Chinese religion and culture which needs to be opened up in order to give a greater understanding of the multitudinous facets of Chinese life. For many Chinese in the world these teachings and the predictions made by diviners like our own colleague Kwok Man Ho are as important as the regular saying of prayers in Islam, the observation of the Sabbath in Judaism or Sunday attendance for Christians. As readers you are not called upon necessarily to agree or disagree with what is stated – no more than if you were to read a book on the prayers of Islam or the Sabbath celebrations in Judaism. What you are asked to do is to recognize that for many people this is a part of the belief which shapes and gives meaning to their lives, as does any belief. We hope that in using this book something of this will be felt and explored.

Lines of Destiny attempts to bring the reader closer to a subject which has a valid place alongside other ancient Chinese sciences. As such it opens up another path which can help Westerners to begin to understand the nature of Chinese popular religion and society.

The wide-ranging material discussed and illustrated in this book is only the tip of the iceberg. Chinese physiognomy goes into enormous detail on all aspects of the human body, enough to provide numerous further books. It is a case of 'look at yourself and read on'!

Notes

CHAPTER 1

1. Donald J. Munro, *The Concept of Man in Early China*, Stanford University Press, 1969, pp. 86–8.
2. *I Ching (The Book of Changes)*, trans. Richard Wilhelm, Routledge & Kegan Paul, 1984.
3. *Shu Ching (The Book of Historical Documents)*, in *The Chinese Classics*, trans. James Legge, Oxford University Press, 1871; Southern Materials Center Inc., Taipai, 1983, vol. III, pp. 138–40.
4. Lao Tzu, *Tao Te Ching*, trans. D. C. Lau, Penguin Books, 1963; Man-jan Chenge, *The Tao Teh Ching*, trans. Tam C. Gibbs, North Atlantic Books, Richmond, California, 1981.
5. *Chuang Tzu*, trans. Herbert A. Giles, Allen & Unwin, 1980.
6. ibid., p. 76.
7. *The Records of the Three Kingdoms*, in Kenneth T. De Woskin, *Doctors, Diviners and Magicians of Ancient China: Biographies of Fang-shih*, Columbia University Press, 1983, pp. 134–7.
8. Adapted from *A Record of Buddhist Kingdoms*, trans. James Legge, Clarendon Press, 1886; Paragon & Dover, 1965, p. 2.
9. J. J. M. De Groot, *The Religious System of China*, Brill, Leiden, 1892, vol. III, p. 957.
10. See note 3 above.
11. *Li Chi (The Record of Rites)*, in *The Sacred Books of the East*, trans. James Legge, Oxford University Press, 1855, vols. XXVII and XVIII.
12. ibid.
13. Martin Palmer (ed.), *T'ung Shu: The Ancient Chinese Almanac*, Rider, 1986.

CHAPTER 2

1. See Stephen Tang and Martin Palmer, *Chinese Herbal Prescriptions*, Rider, 1986, Introduction.
2. De Woskin, op. cit., p. 3.
3. Ssu-ma Ch'ien, *Shih Chi (The Records of the Historian)*; the section referred to is taken from the Chinese edition.
4. 'The Book of Chow', *Shu Ching*, part V, book XIX, para. 2, in *The Chinese Classics*, vol. III, p. 511.

5. Ssu-ma Ch'ien, op. cit.
6. ibid., 'The Biography of Ts'ai Tse'.
7. *Hsun Tzu*, in Henri Doré, *Researches into Chinese Superstitions*, 15 vols., Walsh, Shanghai, 1914.
8. Lo Kuan-chung, *The Romance of the Three Kingdoms* (*San Kuo Chih Yen-I*), edited by C. H. Brewitt-Taylor, Charles E. Tuttle, Japan, 1959.
9. Doré, op cit.
10. C. K. Yang, *Religion in Chinese Society*, University of California Press, 1967, p. 261.
11. English translation from *Religion in the People's Republic of China*, Documentation no. 11, 1963.

CHAPTER 3

1. *Fung Kam*, edited by Li Hing Chit, Mon Wen Publishers, Hong Kong (Chinese edition).